Praise for *Nourish*

"We are all so hungry for authentic faith, and that's what NOURISH provides. Katie's raw transparency transforms us, pointing us to the power of the living, breathing, active Word of God. Draw deeply on the truth found in these pages. Discover health for your body, mind, and soul that you knew was out there, but is now at your very fingertips."

—Eileen Wilder, best-selling author of
The Brave Body Method

"Katie Farrell has gifted us with both an encouraging pep talk and a powerful tool tucked away in the pages of NOURISH. Full of relatable real-life stories and laced with relevant scriptures, this practical book beautifully unearths the intrinsic connection between the body, soul, and spirit and gives us useful advice for tending to all three of them in a way that glorifies God."

—Karen Ehman, Proverbs 31 Ministries speaker and
New York Times best-selling author of *Keep It Shut:*
What to Say, How to Say It, and When to Say Nothing
at All and *Listen, Love, Repeat: Other-Centered Living*
in a Self-Centered World, wife and mother of three

"NOURISH is a powerful resource of truth in action. Katie does a beautiful job of moving from a biblical foundation to practical application. You will be blessed by her transparency, her wisdom, and of course, her recipes. I can't wait to watch God use this book!"

—Michelle Myers, founder of She Works His Way
and Cross Training Couture

"In a culture that leaves us starving for more, Katie's Farrell's latest book, NOURISH, is true to its title. Every chapter and every word leaves your soul satisfied and I truly believe it is Katie's most authentic piece of work. Starting with her own struggle with identity and a draining eating disorder, there is no doubt her guidance and encouragement in the following chapters are rooted in empathetic love. She has found the secret to achieving self-acceptance, believing completely in God's Word, and she walks you through unleashing its power in your life. This book is for every woman (and man) in every shape and size. The information is spiritually rich and so practical you can apply it that day...not to mention the delicious recipes at the end of every chapter. Katie is kind and her words are patient. If you are looking for lasting change in your walk with wellness, pick up this book and be nourished."

—Leslee Owen, television producer

"As someone with my own personal journey with food addiction and a subsequent weight-loss journey, I found the recipes in NOURISH to be healthy and satisfying, but even more so, Katie's words are satisfying to the heart! Katie strikes the perfect balance of spiritual insight, practical advice for growing in one's faith, and encouragement for all of us on a journey to better health and well-being in our lives. I found NOURISH to be true nourishment for my soul!"

—Heather Patterson, coauthor of
Life in Season and *At the Picket Fence*

"As a model and fitness expert for more than a decade I know all too well about body image issues and unhealthy relationships with food. As a Christian, it certainly hasn't escaped me that the very magazines I am featured in and on perpetuate an ideal that many women feel burdened to achieve. With NOURISH, Katie encourages us all to dive into God's Word and discover His truths for our lives. Having wrestled with food and body image issues, being both overweight and underweight, Katie shares her personal testimony of how her relationship with God freed her from the burden to meet the ideals of the world, and she lovingly shares with an open heart how you and I can do that in our own lives. She offers scripture, questions to ponder, prayers, and recipes throughout the book like a best friend who is right there with you, lifting you up out of the trenches. If you've ever struggled or know someone who has struggled with self-worth and feels like their only value is wrapped up in their appearance, pick up this book and let Katie help remind you how uniquely created and deeply treasured you truly are."

—Jamie Eason Middleton, fitness expert, cover model, author, and cocreator of Lean Body for Her

"Katie's raw vulnerability in sharing her story is a powerful testimony of God capturing a woman's heart and transforming her completely. Her story is relatable and inspiring, guaranteed to encourage and nourish those who read it."

—Jennifer Smith, author of *The Unveiled Wife: Embracing Intimacy with God and Your Husband* and *Wife after God: Drawing Closer to God & Your Husband*

Nourish

Discover God's Perfectly Balanced
Plan for Your Body and Soul

Katie Farrell, RN

New York • Nashville

Copyright © 2017 by Katie Farrell, RN

Cover design by Brand Navigation
Cover photography by Heather Jowett
Cover copyright © 2017 by Hachette Book Group, Inc.

FaithWords
Hachette Book Group
1290 Avenue of the Americas, New York, NY 10104
faithwords.com
twitter.com/faithwords

First Edition: December 2017

FaithWords is a division of Hachette Book Group, Inc. The FaithWords name and logo are trademarks of Hachette Book Group, Inc.

The publisher is not responsible for websites (or their content) that are not owned by the publisher.

The Hachette Speakers Bureau provides a wide range of authors for speaking events. To find out more, go to www.hachettespeakersbureau.com or call (866) 376-6591.

Library of Congress Control Number: 2017952593

ISBN: 978-1-4789-7606-6 (hardcover), 978-1-4789-7605-9 (ebook)

Printed in the United States of America

LSC-C

10 9 8 7 6 5 4 3 2 1

*To Jesus Christ, my Savior, Heavenly Father, and closest friend.
Thank You for how You satisfy the deepest parts of my soul
with Your great love. Thank You for Your Word, which transforms
us. To my incredible husband, Sean, thank you for loving,
supporting, and cheering me on every step of the way.
I love sharing this journey called life with you. You are a gift,
and my best friend. To my daughter, Madeline Joy,
as I wrote this book God was knitting you together in
my womb. You are my precious treasure from the Lord
and my beauty from ashes.*

CONTENTS

1. Beauty for Ashes 1

2. Freedom from Weight 21

3. Nourishing the Soul 37

4. What's in Your Garden? 47

5. Bearing Fruit That Will Last 69

6. Strengthening Your Spiritual Muscles 81

7. Nourishing the Body 97

8. Putting It All into Practice 113

9. Changing Your Focus of Food 131

10. Strength to Run Your Race 155

11. Enjoy the Journey 173

Appendix 1. Lies Versus Truth Chart 187

Appendix 2. Scripture-Based Prayers for Your Identity in Christ 189

Acknowledgments 193

About the Author 195

Nourish

1

BEAUTY FOR ASHES

*I*t was the summer of 1998. I was fourteen years old when my dad came to my two sisters and me and informed us that we would be moving from the only home we had ever known, in suburban Michigan, to a small town in Wisconsin. My dad worked as an administrator for a small health-care agency that was experiencing layoffs, forcing him to find a new job.

This kind of news would be shocking to any teenager, but even more so to a shy fourteen-year-old about to enter her first year of high school. My parents sat us down and told us that we would have just a few weeks to say goodbye to the only home, school, and friends we had ever known.

A New Beginning

After just a few weeks, we packed our suitcases and family of five into our minivan and began the eight-hour ride to a small rental we would soon call home. Tears were shed from the moment we left our home in Troy, Michigan (population 70,000), until we pulled into our new hometown, Shawano, Wisconsin (population 7,000).

I will never forget the scene as we pulled into the driveway of our small, unfurnished rental home. The surrounding area had

1

a skate park, one gas station, and a small convenience store. This was a huge difference from being within walking distance of one of Michigan's largest malls, multiple grocery stores, and every chain store imaginable. As you can imagine, all these changes meant quite the culture shock for my teen sisters and me.

A Single Lie Breeds Destruction

After what had seemed to be the longest summer of my life, the start of the new school year finally approached. I remember walking into the high school with sweaty palms, making my way down the endless hallway to find my locker. I headed to my first classes of the day and sat quietly in the back. Suddenly the lunch bell rang, and I realized I had survived the morning only to have the real nerves kick in.

Lunch period was always nerve racking for me on the first day of school, but it was taken to a whole new level when I was the new kid. I remember walking through the noisy lunchroom, slowly wandering past the first table...and the next, anxiously wondering where I should set down my lunch tray. I spotted a table that seemed to be open, so I made my way over.

As I was walking toward the table, a boy I recognized from one of my classes started to walk toward me. When he approached me, he handed me a folded piece of paper and said, "This is for you." I wasn't quite sure what to expect... Was the note from him or one of his friends? Was he going to ask me a question, or could it be possible that he had a crush on me? It seemed hundreds of questions raced through my mind as I unfolded the paper.

I nervously opened the folds, only to expose a grotesque

image of an overweight female with disproportionate body parts. Immediately the boy started laughing, and said, "Just in case you didn't know, this is what you look like." Just as soon as he spoke those words, he turned and ran back to the table where his friends sat laughing.

In a state of shock and embarrassment, I dropped the paper, threw down my lunch tray, and ran to the bathroom, where I locked myself in a stall and cried for what seemed like an eternity. I was humiliated and I didn't see how I could ever leave the bathroom, much less return to the lunchroom.

It was at that moment that I went from being carefree about my appearance to being hyperaware of how my body looked. Although giving me that drawing was most likely nothing more than a cruel joke to those young men, I can look back and perceive it as something much deeper. I can now see how this single event was set up by the enemy to steal my innocence and identity by planting a lie in my mind.

Although I had grown up in a Christian home, and asked Jesus to be my Lord and Savior at an early age, the revelation of who I was in Christ had not yet been revealed to me. This left me open to the lies of the enemy, most of which were specifically targeted at my identity. This single lie, when fostered and meditated on, eventually took root in my life, leading me down a road of eating disorders that lasted the majority of my teen years.

A Desperate Attempt to Obtain Control

Soon after that lunch event, I convinced myself I had to lose weight, and fast, despite the fact that I was at a healthy weight at the time. It was almost as if I went overnight from being carefree about food to trying every diet and weight-loss trick. Within a few weeks I went from three healthy meals a day to a granola bar for breakfast, a dry turkey sandwich for lunch, and a few bites of food at dinner—just so my mom wouldn't catch on to my new eating habits.

I continued to cut back on the little food I was eating with each passing week. And as my food consumption gradually decreased, so did my appetite and weight. My clothes got looser, and I felt empowered, knowing my plan was working.

With the weight loss came a sense of control. I believed that my changing body would protect me from the rejection I had experienced in that lunchroom. I convinced myself that if I could maintain a state of "perfection" in the way I looked, I would always be accepted and loved by those around me.

One single lie that I had received planted a seed in the soil of my heart. Left to itself, it grew and spread like the weed it was, resulting in a series of lies that played over and over inside my head. The problem was that I didn't know I was believing a lie, or that I was harming myself and my body. At that time I was completely and utterly deceived. It would never have crossed my mind that I was heading down the road of an eating disorder in the form of anorexia nervosa.

Time for an Intervention

I wasn't the only one who noticed I'd lost a substantial amount of weight. I tried to hide my behavior from my mom, but it wasn't long before she became aware that something was wrong. When I asked my mom to recount the day she became suspicious of an eating disorder, she replied that she remembers it perfectly: "It was an early winter day and we had decided to go clothes shopping for the coming season. When I came into the dressing room to check how a pair of jeans fit on you, I lifted your shirt to check the fit of the waistband. I recall seeing your ribs and hip bones protruding from your dwindling frame, and at that moment I knew something was terribly wrong. I walked out of the dressing room, silently shocked to see how much weight you had lost. I began to wonder how it happened without me knowing it. How had you gone from a beautiful, healthy teenager to an insecure young woman who was hiding something behind her malnourished body?"

Looking back, my mom recalls noticing that I was eating a little less at dinner. Yet I had managed to convince her I was eating more at school, which explained why I wasn't as hungry in the evening. Despite my efforts to hide my behavior, she had a hard realization of the truth when she saw my bony body in the dressing room that day.

In the weeks to follow, I remember my mom bringing up my eating habits in subtle ways. Her tactics didn't get very far, though, because, as is common with teenagers, I became very defensive. After many failed attempts to expose the truth, my mom eventually got my dad involved. I could tell my parents were getting serious when they forced me to step on the scale. I weighed a mere eighty-five pounds. It was then they decided I needed professional help.

Days later, my mom and dad took me to our family physician, who clearly didn't specialize in eating disorders: he joked about how I could stand to eat a few hamburgers and needed to gain some weight, then sent me on my way. My parents' next line of defense was to have me see a Christian counselor, which I was not in favor of. I remember thinking to myself, *I will not share the private details of my life with a stranger!* So I sat on her couch defiantly, responding with one-word answers or not at all. As you can imagine, these appointments didn't last very long, and eventually the counselor told my parents that I would have to come back when I was ready to share. My parents hesitantly brought me home from that appointment and decided to start doing the one thing they knew to do: pray.

A Promise of Hope

As winter turned to spring, I started to take walks down a path near our Wisconsin home. These walks started off as an effort to burn additional calories, but I could sense that something deeper was taking place in my heart as the trees began to bud and eventually blossom.

It was on one of those walks that I noticed a butterfly swirling and twirling around me, almost as if it were following me. This wasn't such a big deal; however, the next day, that very same butterfly came and met me on my walk again. It happened again and again, day after day, until suddenly I started to think, *What if this butterfly is a sign from God? What if He is using it to try to tell me something?*

If there was any chance at all that this butterfly could be a sign from God, I knew I couldn't ignore it. So I went home and began to do as much research as I could about butterflies. During my search I also asked God to show me in His Word if there was any reference to what He was trying to show me through these butterflies.

As I began to flip through the pages of my Bible, one Scripture stood out to me that paired perfectly with my new-found knowledge of butterflies. That verse was Romans 12:2: "Don't copy the behavior and customs of this world, but let God transform you into a new person by changing the way you think. Then you will learn to know God's will for you, which is good and pleasing and perfect." As I read this passage, the word *transform* seemed to jump off the page, as it was one of the words that described the transition from a caterpillar to a butterfly. I wrote this Scripture down in my journal and tucked it away in my heart, not knowing exactly what it meant yet, but knowing that it was a part of God's promise to me.

A New Chapter

Just a few months into the summer my dad got word that a job in Michigan had opened up, just about an hour from where I'd grown up. He asked the rest of the family if we were open to the idea of moving back to Michigan. We were all so excited at the thought of moving back home, he didn't waste any time and quickly took the job interview. Just a few days later my dad got word that he got the job. And so we found ourselves packing boxes all over again, just two short years after our move to Wisconsin.

Our move back to Michigan brought us to a quaint town called Saline. The culture of Saline fell somewhere between the big city we'd grown up in and the rural farmlands of Wisconsin. Needless to say, it didn't take long to feel like home! I knew things would be different in Saline when my first day of school brought a handful of new friends, as well as an invitation to sit with some of them at lunch. Within a few weeks, I felt as if I fit in for the first time in years!

With the approach of the fall season came Saline's homecoming. Being that I was still one of the new girls at the school, I was ecstatic when I was invited by a group of friends to attend the homecoming dance. At that dance one of my friends introduced me to a boy named Sean, and we quickly hit it off. We hit it off so well, in fact, that I spent the rest of the night talking to Sean rather than dancing with my friends. At the end of the night, Sean and I agreed that we should exchange phone numbers, knowing we could talk for hours.

Sean called me the very next day, and we spent close to three hours on the phone. Although we had just met, it felt as if we had known each other forever. At the end of the conversation, Sean asked me if I would like to go on a date, and I replied nervously, "Yes." (Little did I know at the time that I was saying yes to a date with my future husband!) Sean and I started officially dating when we were just sixteen, and it didn't take long for us to become best friends and high school sweethearts.

Disorder Takes on a Different Form

It was such a relief to feel that I was finally in a place I could call home. It wasn't long before my peace within began to reflect outwardly. I soon began to gain weight steadily, which put my parents at ease. They took my increasing weight as a sign that all was well at last.

Everything seemed to be going right in my life at that time, and I truly felt that I was on cloud nine! I had a steady boyfriend and a great group of girlfriends, and I was doing well in school. My emotions were at an all-time high, and my eating habits soon began to match my enjoyment. The only problem was that I had no proper knowledge of nutrition, and it didn't take long for the pounds to creep back on...and then some.

My expanding waistline brought back feelings of anxiety as I became increasingly aware of my body yet again. I began to feel a sense of panic. It seemed I was losing control. Looking back, I now see how dangerous this mind-set was. I have come to learn that when we do anything out of fear, we give the enemy an open door to our lives.

I began to look for methods for losing weight; and sure enough, the enemy made sure that I found one. One evening as I was alone watching a Lifetime movie, I found the "solution" I was looking for.

In the movie a bunch of girls were having a slumber party, and were snacking on some junk food. During the sleepover, two of the girls were discussing their fear of getting fat; to which one of them said, "You can eat whatever you want without gaining weight. All you have to do is throw up after eating." She then proceeded to explain how to self-induce vomiting.

This scene painted a somewhat glamorous picture of bulimia in my mind, but to be honest, I was scared to actually try it. That is, until the fear of gaining more weight superseded the fear of this grotesque action.

I will never forget the first time I self-induced vomiting. I had just come home from school and found a pan of brownies sitting on the stove. I took one look at those brownies and thought, *Instead of eating just one, why not enjoy the whole pan and then get rid of it shortly after?* I called out for my mom and sisters to make sure I had the house to myself. Sure enough, no one else was home.

I decided that it was safe to follow through with my plan, so I went ahead and ate the entire pan of brownies; I barely took a moment to catch my breath, much less actually taste them. Just as quickly as I had eaten the brownies, I ran to the bathroom to get rid of them. I remember feeling mostly numb during the binge/purge cycle, and also a bit excited about how "easy" it was to get rid of the calories I had just consumed. This was my first step down the road to bulimia—lasting a total of two years. In those years my weight fluctuated (if anything I gained weight as a result of my binges), and I ate normal meals throughout the day, so it was easy to keep my actions a secret. Or so I thought.

I'm Finally Free

I celebrated my eighteenth birthday with dinner and an ice cream cake, as was the tradition in my family. After indulging in a large slice of cake, I sneaked away to the bathroom to purge. To my surprise, when I opened the door to the bathroom, my younger sister, Emily, was waiting for me. She asked to talk to me privately in her bedroom. As I walked into Emily's room, I saw my older sister, Sarah, sitting on the bed. My heart started racing. I knew my sisters were sitting me down for a serious talk.

I sat on the bed and watched tears begin to run down my sisters' faces as they proceeded to share their hearts with me. "We know what you have been doing," Sarah said.

"What do you mean?" I replied nervously, the blood rushing to my face and my palms starting to sweat.

"We know what you have been doing in the bathroom. And we are scared you'll hurt yourself if you keep this up," Emily mumbled amid her tears.

Just as quickly as she said those words, tears started streaming down my face. I was exposed—my secrets revealed. I felt incredibly ashamed. My shame lasted for only a brief moment, however, because my sisters' next words were, "Let's pray." With those words we joined hands and prayed together a prayer that was one of the most memorable and powerful of my life. My sisters took turns praying over my heart, mind, and body, asking God to restore, heal, and set me free in these areas. I also repented for the years I had neglected and abused my body, and made a dedication of my health to the Lord that evening.

With a single prayer I knew God had done a work in my heart, and I would never be the same. I could feel God breaking chains that had me bound for years. I felt the guilt and shame run off me as if I were taking a refreshing shower. God's presence filled that room. Within an instant I perceived that I had been supernaturally delivered from any and all desires to binge, purge, or restrict food from myself. That night I was shaken to the core, not only emotionally (from seeing my sisters so brokenhearted for me), but also spiritually as my Savior, Jesus Christ, redeemed me from my sin.

After this profound experience, I quickly learned that when we call out to Jesus for deliverance, He instantly washes our sins away, and sets us free from the chains that had us bound. From there our minds still need to be renewed and restored, which can be a process. In my case, I had spent years entertaining destructive thoughts in relation to my body and food, and although I was freed of my outward actions, I still had to be healed on the inside. I wasn't quite sure how to go about this, but I knew that God was the author of my healing and that He would be faithful to finish the work He had started in me.

My Search for Healing Begins

My search for inner healing began the very next day as I lay on my bed and cried out to the Lord. I asked Him to show me how to change my way of thinking and heal the wounds in my heart. I grabbed my Bible off the nightstand, hoping to find the answer I had been looking for. To my surprise I opened my Bible directly to Romans 12:2, "Don't copy the behavior and customs of this world, but let God transform you into a new person by changing the way you think. Then you will learn to know God's will for you, which is good and pleasing and perfect." In that moment I was confronted yet again with the word *transform*, which confirmed that it was the key to my healing.

I desperately needed a transformation on the inside, and this Scripture provided a road map for getting there. It stated that if I wanted lasting change, I would have to make the choice to be different from the rest of this world and dig into God's Word like never before. The discovery of Romans 12:2 was so simple, yet it was profound enough to change my destiny. From that moment on, I got serious about God's Word, studying it every chance I got.

I began nursing school just a few months later at a campus near my house. I was so hungry for the Word of God that I found myself listening to an audio version of the Bible in my car during my commute to school. I would bring my Bible to school, reading it in between classes and during my break. As I prayed and spent time with the Lord, the entrance of God's Word brought light where there had been darkness, and His truth began to expose the lies.

As I progressed through nursing school, I developed a whole new appreciation for the human body. My eyes were opened to what a gift our bodies are, and I realized how vital it is that we care for them properly. In doing so we are not only thinking about our health, we are also thanking God for the precious temple He has given us! This revelation, in combination with God's Word, brought forth a total renewal of my mind and heart.

In addition to my being changed on the inside, God started to do a powerful transformation on the outside. This change began when I got in the kitchen and started cooking. I started to learn to make healthier versions of foods I had once enjoyed. Unlike those who learn to cook from a person close to them, I like to think that God was the one Who taught me how to cook. I believe He inspired me to get into the kitchen and gave me the wisdom and ability to create recipes. Looking back, I see that this was an essential part of my healing while I formed a new, healthy relationship with food. Within a few months of my spending time in the kitchen, God had exchanged my fears and need for control for a sense of freedom, balance, and true enjoyment when it came to food.

Little by little I started seeing change emerge in my heart, and it was then that God brought back the image of the butterfly to my mind. I remember reading about caterpillars and how they make their transformation inside the cocoon. After the process is complete, a beautiful butterfly emerges. God brought the revelation of the butterfly full circle as my own transformation took place. He revealed to me that as with the caterpillar, it was in the secret place where I would spend quiet time with Him that my transformation would occur. Before I knew it, I had gone from an earthbound caterpillar to a butterfly that could soar above the cares and the troubles of this world—all because of the time I spent in God's presence, which renewed and restored me from the inside out.

New Beginnings

After graduating from nursing school, I went on to marry my high school sweetheart, Sean, at the age of twenty-four. After graduating from Eastern Michigan University, I got my first job as a labor and delivery nurse, which had been a dream of mine since I was a little girl. One of my favorite things about being a L&D nurse was that I had the opportunity to work one-on-one with women. This allowed me to get to know my patients personally, which opened the door for many teaching opportunities. I quickly found that one of my favorite things to teach women was how nutrition would affect their recovery after having a baby.

I would come home from work on countless days and share my excitement with Sean about what I had been able to teach my patients. Since Sean was a graphic designer, he encouraged me to start a website where I could share my nutrition tips, recipes, and also what God had taught me over the years about how to care for our bodies. I thought that sounded like a great idea, and just as quickly as I agreed, he was off to create a website for me! Just a few days later, my sister, my husband, and I were discussing what to name the website. Collectively we came up with the name Dashing Dish, and the website was born!

Within just six months of launching the website, I was getting more feedback than I could have imagined about how Dashing Dish was changing people's lives! I started to realize the great responsibility God had given me with this website and that it was meant to share much more than just recipes. I felt the Lord prompting me to share about the freedom and joy that could be found only in Him, and to teach women how to find their true beauty in exchange for the ashes of their life. After a few years I came to a place where I knew beyond a shadow of a doubt God was calling me to step into Dashing Dish full-time, as both a ministry and a business.

Yet, despite knowing God was calling me, I started to have my doubts. How could I have spent five long years in nursing school and have the job of my dreams and give it all up for something that hadn't even been established as an official business or ministry yet? I began to wrestle with what my heart was telling me, and I second-guessed myself every time I gave way to my doubts. Although it didn't make sense to me at the time, the Lord began to calm my thoughts with His Word. I began to think back on the years that I had struggled with an unhealthy relationship with my body and food and how God had set me free. I knew that if He'd done it for me, He also wanted to do it for many others, and He was calling me to be a vehicle to bring freedom.

Despite my fears, I decided to listen to my heart and trust His plan. I spent many months thinking over my decision and talking to my husband, my parents, and many godly mentors whom I respect. God used every single person to confirm that this was indeed God's call on my life. It was then that I knew it was time to leave the security of my nursing job and jump full-time into the ministry that He was calling me to. On August 9, 2011, I decided to step out in obedience and follow God's leading. It certainly felt like stepping out of the boat. However, I have found that when I make the decision to step out in faith, God never lets me sink, as long as I keep my eyes on Him.

On the day that I left my nursing job, God led me to 2 Timothy 4:5. It reads, "But you should keep a clear mind in every situation. Don't be afraid of suffering for the Lord. Work at telling others the Good News, and fully carry out the ministry God has given you." I knew that by making that decision, I had taken the first step in pursuing the ministry God had called me to. I made the decision to pour out my life as an offering to God. And how could I not after Jesus had given His life for me?

God was about to lead me to a ministry that was far beyond myself! While I was switching over to Dashing Dish full-time, God began to flood my mind with ways that I could minister to people. He placed a deep desire within me to provide practical resources such as recipes and meal-planning tools and combine them with encouragement that would bring health to the soul. From the very beginning God led me to encourage the readers of Dashing Dish to pursue health on a heart level, which would then bring change from the inside out.

Beauty for Ashes

As I sit and write this book, I can honestly say that there isn't a single area of my life that God hasn't restored. One powerful example of His restoration is that I am currently pregnant with our first child, a little girl we have named Madeline Joy. When I got pregnant, doctors were shocked. It was something I was told might never happen after the abuse that I'd put my body through for so many years. But with God...all things are possible (see Matt. 19:26 NIV). I could write a book just on how faithful God has been in redeeming all that was lost! He truly has taken the ashes of my life and turned them into something beautiful.

I share my story not only to bring God glory, but also to encourage you. No matter where you may find yourself today or what you are going through, I believe the answer can be found in Jesus! As you read my story you may relate to having an unhealthy relationship with your body or food, or perhaps you simply want to start eating healthier. If that's the case, I believe God has an answer for nourishing your body.

On the other hand, maybe you find yourself going through something that isn't related to food or your body at all, but instead is weighing you down emotionally. If you can relate to feeling burdened by the cares of this life, I believe God has a plan for nourishing your soul as well!

As you go through this book, it is my prayer that God will use what He has shown me over the years to set you free from the things that weigh you down. As we take this journey together, I would encourage you to pray and ask God to help you discover His *perfectly balanced plan for your body and soul.* I firmly believe that God wants to take the ashes of each one of our lives and turn them into something beautiful!

FOOD FOR THOUGHT

Nourishment for the Soul

Scripture

To all who mourn in Israel, he will give a crown of beauty for ashes, a joyous blessing instead of mourning, festive praise instead of despair (Isa. 61:3).

Reflection Questions

- Can you identify with having an unhealthy relationship with your body and/or food? If so, where do you think these issues first began?
- What are some things in your life that are weighing you down emotionally? If you were to break free from these burdens, how would your life change overall?

Prayer

Dear Lord, I thank You that You are the one Who knit me together in my mother's womb, and all my days were written in Your book before one of them ever came to be. You know everything that I have gone through in my past, and You know everything that I am going through now. I ask You to walk with me through this journey, Father, and to show me the areas of my life that need a touch from You. I thank You that You are the great restorer, and that You are able to take the ashes of my life and turn them into something beautiful. Please help me to discover what Your perfect plan is for my body and soul. In Jesus' Name, amen.

Nourishment for the Body

Baked Oatmeal Singles

Breakfast is the most important meal of the day, but for most people it is also the busiest time of day. If you love the idea of oatmeal for breakfast but simply don't have the time, this is the perfect breakfast for you! These baked oatmeal singles are perfectly portioned, and they are great cold, warm, or on the go. They make a wonderful pre- or postworkout snack as well.

Ingredients

Cooking spray
2 cups old-fashioned oats
½ cup vanilla or plain protein powder
1½ teaspoons baking powder
1 teaspoon salt
¼ cup baking stevia (or sweetener to taste)
¼ cup maple syrup or honey
1 large egg

1 large egg white
½ cup unsweetened applesauce
½ cup plain low-fat Greek yogurt (or 1 mashed banana)
¼ cup chocolate chips (optional)
½ teaspoon cinnamon

Method

Preheat the oven to 350°F. Spray a muffin tin with cooking spray (or line with foil liners sprayed with cooking spray, or parchment liners).

Combine all ingredients in a large bowl, stirring until combined. Stir in the chocolate chips or sprinkle them on top, if desired.

Divide the oatmeal mixture evenly among the prepared muffin tins. Bake uncovered for 20 to 25 minutes or until oatmeal is lightly browned and a toothpick comes out clean. Store in the fridge until ready to eat.

Yields: 12 servings

2

FREEDOM FROM WEIGHT

*B*efore we embark on the rest of this journey together, I want you to take a moment and let one simple but profound truth sink in. In fact, I want you to pray and ask God to reveal this truth to you, because it really is the foundation for the rest of what I will be sharing, and it could become a pivotal revelation if you fully grasp it. *God wants you to be free from everything that weighs you down, spiritually, physically, and emotionally.*

He isn't just interested in your spiritual health and eternal salvation, He cares about your body and emotions as well! He cares so much, in fact, that He wants nothing more than to be invited into these areas of your life so He can guide and direct you to the place of peace and freedom He has provided for you.

We can be sure of this, because we have God's Word to confirm it. 1 Thessalonians 5:23 shares God's heart on the matter: "Now may the God of peace make you holy in every way, and may your whole spirit and soul and body be kept blameless until our Lord Jesus Christ comes again." We can see in this passage that the God of peace Himself wants to sanctify (which means to purify, free from sin, or unburden) every part of our being.

Maybe this is a new revelation to you and it's the first time you have ever heard or even thought about the fact that God cares for you deeply. Or perhaps you know that God is good and that He cares about your eternal redemption, but it's never occurred to you that He wants to be involved in every area of your life.

Either way, when you stop and think about it, this really should be common sense! Just think, if God took the time to knit every part of your body together, giving you talents, personality, and emotions that are unique to you, why wouldn't He want to be involved in all of them?

Carrying Our Burdens

If this is an obvious fact, why is it that so many of us find it hard to trust God with our bodies, thoughts, and emotions? When we finally make the choice to give our cares and burdens to the Lord, why do we pick them back up again moments later? I believe this trouble comes from the fact that we have a *mental* knowledge of God's involvement in our lives, but we haven't let the revelation of how much He loves us sink down to a heart level.

This lack of understanding puts us in a self-willed mentality that leaves us feeling worn out and frustrated as we carry around the weight of things we were never intended to carry. I remember when I found this to be true in my own life. Just as I described in my testimony, I spent years going from one extreme to another, trying to control my surroundings. Although I grew up knowing Jesus as my Savior, I found myself conforming to the world's way of doing things, which left me unfulfilled, exhausted, and unhealthy.

Even though I knew God loved me, I struggled to surrender

my body to Him, in addition to many other areas of my life. My tight grip was a direct result of my lack of trust in His care for me. After all, if I had truly trusted that His plan was better than my own, I would have been more willing to surrender my all to Him.

The Source of Our Problem Is Dependence on Self

Have you ever been where I was? I think most have. Over the years I have talked to and worked with countless women who are being consumed with these very struggles. Although so many of them knew Jesus as Savior, they shared their struggle to come to Him with open hands and an open heart.

I began to ask myself, "Why are all these incredible women, who are successful mothers, business owners, and entrepreneurs, allowing things like losing the last five pounds and winning others' approval steal the fullness of what God has for them?" One day I was standing in the checkout lane at the grocery store when my eyes landed on a cover of a magazine that said, "ACHIEVE YOUR BEST BODY NOW" in big bold letters across the cover.

It was then that it hit me! I realized that on any given day, we could be doing something as innocent as buying groceries, and within a matter of moments be bombarded with words and images that encourage us to rely on our own efforts. These images tell us that our worth and value as a woman are found in our appearance, and that with enough determination and perseverance, we can finally achieve the airbrushed body we see on the cover.

Even more, the word *now* stood out to me. I began to

consider how the media influences our society, which has a quick fix for everything. If you are hungry, for example, you can just pop a meal in the microwave for one minute, and voila, you have a meal! Most of the messages we are being bombarded with are promises to give extraordinary results with little work and time.

As I glanced over the rest of the magazine covers, I noticed something else: the ever-present pressure to diet. I stood there and thought, *It's no wonder so many women have an unhealthy relationship with food and their bodies!* The worst part of all is that these messages are so prevalent, most of us have become desensitized to them. What's more, all these extreme diets and false promises of happiness are the perfect example of the way our culture functions: it is always changing. As I stood there I noticed that two magazines sitting side by side had messages on their covers that completely contradicted one another. One magazine claimed that eating low-carb was the answer to weight-loss victory, while the next guaranteed that a low-calorie diet was the best way to go.

Yet despite the fact that the claims made by these magazines are often unrealistic and contradictory, they continue to sell by the millions. This tells me one thing: people are desperately looking for guidance on caring for their bodies. There is just one problem with all these diets, plans, and formulas: each one encourages us to rely on our own strength and ability. I believe that this is the opposite of how God designed us, which is to completely rely upon Him in every area of our lives. It's no wonder every cheap imitation we settle for always seems to fall short.

I left the grocery store that day with a heavy heart, but

it got me thinking. All the messages that we are bombarded with daily can leave any one of us feeling overwhelmed and confused, unsure of where to turn. I began to see why so many of us have trouble surrendering to the Lord. In the midst of all the noise, how often are we tuning in to His leading?

I believe that if we are ever going to experience lasting freedom in the way we view our bodies, food, and anything else that weighs us down, we have to look to the One Who is constant, Who *never* changes.

Freedom in Surrender

Are you ready to ditch the diets and surrender everything to God? If so, I'm going to let you in on a little secret. God's way of doing things is often different from the world's. But so are His results! His way also takes time and effort on our part, but His way comes with lasting transformation that leads to freedom.

Now, your next thought may be, *Where do I begin?* Well, I'm glad you asked! Let's go back to the beginning of this chapter, when I told you that God wants you to be free from everything that weighs you down, spiritually, physically, and emotionally. I believe this single idea, when understood on a heart level, is our starting point to begin fully depending on God.

Psalm 62:5–8 paints a beautiful picture of what happens when we stop relying on ourselves and start depending on God. It says, "Let all that I am wait quietly before God, for my hope is in him. He alone is my rock and my salvation, my fortress where I will not be shaken. My victory and honor come from God alone. He is my refuge, a rock where no enemy can reach me. O my people, trust in him at all times. Pour out your heart to him, for God is our refuge." This is just one of the hundreds (if not thousands) of Scriptures that encourage us to place our trust in God and pour our hearts out to Him, for it is there that we find the refuge we seek.

When we grasp the fact that God almighty, the maker of heaven and earth, loves us so deeply that He wants to be involved in the details of our lives, we can breathe a sigh of relief. We are suddenly given permission to release our emotional cares and physical shortcomings to Him, rather than trying to fix them on our own. This frees us from the need to keep all the plates in our lives spinning perfectly, because we can trust that He will guide and support us when we make Him our refuge.

Fellowship with God

Taking this revelation and making it come alive in our hearts is simple, but as I said, it also takes effort on our part. This heart change can happen only when God unveils this truth to us, so the effort begins by spending quality time with Him every day. As we spend time with our Heavenly Father, we will get to know His heart toward us and learn how much He loves us. This may not seem to correlate with our being freed from unwanted weight (whether it be physical or emotional), but it really is the foundation for everything in God's Kingdom.

One way we can spend time with God is by reading the Bible (which is God's Word to us). As we do, the Holy Spirit (our teacher and counselor—see John 14:26) is able to bring it alive to us, which brings revelation. It is then that God is able to speak to us on a heart level and uncover the depths of His love toward us.

Another powerful way we can connect with God is through prayer and praise. This brings us into God's presence. There we will start to develop an intimate relationship with Him, allowing Him to change us on a heart level. Prayer is one of the key ways we can have fellowship with God, as it allows us to communicate and share our hearts with Him. Worship is also essential to understanding His love for us, because it causes us to reflect on the goodness of God. Our fellowship with God is designed to draw us closer to Him, and as we do He promises to draw near to us (see James 4:8).

Just as in any good relationship, the more time we spend with our Heavenly Father, the more our trust and love for Him deepens. The more we trust Him, the more willing we are to submit every area of our life to Him. Drawing closer to God sets off a chain reaction that leads to our complete and total surrender. In this profound moment, it is then that we learn to lay everything at His feet.

He Cares about the Details

As I previously mentioned, I am currently just weeks away from expecting our first child, Madeline Joy. The moment I found out I was pregnant, I was instantly filled with the deepest love for my daughter, who was barely the size of an apple seed at the time. Now that she is the size of a butternut squash, I am more aware of her than ever. As she squirms, kicks, and hiccups in my belly, I can't help but think about what a miracle she is!

It is truly hard to comprehend how God formed each one of us with lungs to help us breathe, a heart that beats, and a personality that is unique...all from a fertilized egg that is smaller than the tip of a pen! Psalm 139 speaks about the time and attention He put into creating each one of us:

> You made all the delicate, inner parts of my body
> and knit me together in my mother's womb.
> Thank you for making me so wonderfully complex!
> Your workmanship is marvelous—how well I
> know it.
> You watched me as I was being formed in utter
> seclusion,
> as I was woven together in the dark of the womb.
> You saw me before I was born.
> Every day of my life was recorded in your book.
> Every moment was laid out
> before a single day had passed. (Psalm 139:13–16)

This passage shows us just how much God loves us—enough that He took the time to design each part of our body, soul, and spirit to fulfill the specific purposes He's created us for. What's even more amazing is that He didn't just create us and leave us to ourselves, but rather, He desires to be involved in our everyday lives!

The more I have gotten to know the Lord over the years, the more aware I am of how He cares about everything that concerns me, no matter how great or small. I always joke that I pray to God for a good hair day every year on my birthday, and it always seems to be my best hair day of all! Although this is a lighthearted example, in all honesty, I have countless stories of how He has proven Himself faithful in both the big and small areas of my life.

So the question is, If He took the time to form us with such precision and care, will we believe that His plan for us is good and trust Him with the details of our lives? Depending on Him isn't always the easiest path, especially when the world offers plenty of distractions along the way, but as we do, we will become the beautiful masterpiece that was designed to bring Him glory!

Surrendering Our Physical Weight

While we are on the topic of releasing our burdens to the Lord, I would be foolish not to address the burden of our physical weight. In fact, I am aware that this topic may be the primary reason you picked up this book. Whether you have been overweight most of your life, you have yo-yoed among thin, average, and obese, or you have always felt that your body is flawed in some other way, God wants to bring you to a place of freedom!

He wants you to be free from the anxieties that arise when you step on the scale or go shopping for clothes.

He wants you to be free from the weight of comparison, worrying what people think, and not measuring up.

He wants you to be free from the burden that is attached to your physical appearance.

But in order to be free, you must surrender these areas to Him, and trust Him with your body.

As we embark on this journey to health together, you will learn practical ways to care for the body God gave you, eventually feeling, working, and even looking better! You will also find that as you care for your body as God intended, your body will settle at the weight for which He originally designed it. I want to mention that this may not be a size 0, and it may mean that you will still see some lumps, curves, and numbers that don't measure up to society's ideal standard of beauty. It will also, however, mean that you are able to live free from the crazy ups and downs that go along with dieting, disordered eating, and the never-ending comparison game.

I can promise that if you surrender your body (which includes your weight, shape, and size) to the Lord, you will find yourself in a place of freedom that you have never felt before! Surrender may look different for everyone, but for me it meant getting rid of my scale for a few years (I now use one to weigh myself about once a month, just to stay on track), and it also meant that I had to learn to love my body wherever my weight naturally settled. For me this number varies slightly depending on hormones, water retention, and the season of life I am in. But for the most part, I have been able to maintain my weight (with a five-pound variance) for about ten years!

I like to think of my body as petite, with some muscle tone (thanks to weight lifting) and some curves (thanks to my genetics). I have learned to love the skin I am in, and most important, I have learned to find my value, worth, and confidence in Christ. In addition, I am learning to appreciate the God-given gift that my body is. Despite that fact that it has been through many highs and lows, it always seems to be forgiving, and it has even been able to bring forth new life, for which I am most thankful!

Being pregnant has also taught me a lot about the beautiful gift of being a woman. Although my body is changing, growing, and stretching in ways I never thought possible, I can see how these changes reveal signs of life within!

Although society might prize a slim silhouette on a woman, the most beautiful thing of all is when our bodies are healthy, strong, and working just as God designed them. This will look a little different on everyone, since each person was created uniquely by Him!

One of my favorite ways to emphasize this truth is to picture ten women lined up next to each other. Now, picture with me how different each one of these women looks from the others. From top to bottom, every woman is extraordinarily unique! From hairstyles to facial features and bodily curves right down to the size of their feet, it is rare to find two women who look exactly the same. Now, compare this to a line of ten men standing side by side. Although there may be some variations in their hair, faces, weights, and heights, I always find that men tend to look pretty similar, especially when it comes to the shape of their bodies. Of course, some guys may have a little more weight in the belly than others, but for the most part they lack the varying curves and unique designs that God gave to women.

This visual may or may not have helped you see your body from a different perspective, but it is my great hope that as you venture through this book, you will be able to see the unique beauty that was given to you by your creator. You, my friend, are God's precious daughter, one of a kind, and so greatly treasured and loved by Him. For that reason alone, you can trust that as you release the care of your physical body, He will bring you to a place of health, freedom, and confidence that can be found only in Him!

Lay Your Burdens Down

One of the things I am most looking forward to after Madeline Joy's birth is watching my husband become a father. I know he will be an amazing dad, because he already is! He is so excited about her arrival, and looks forward to being able to talk to her every day. He is already busy thinking about ways he can provide for her, care for her, and love her, and he prays for her daily. As I watch my husband anticipating the moment that he becomes a dad, I can't help but think about how our Heavenly Father loves us, knowing that not only are we His children, but He is the very one Who fashioned and formed us from the beginning!

Whether you have experienced this kind of love for a child of your own, or you have a wholehearted love for a spouse, a family member, or even a friend, most of us know what it is to love someone deeply. Now think about what you would do for that person and all the ways you think about them, show them love, and care for them daily. Now think about how God, the maker of the universe, values us as His children (see 1 John 3:1).

When I think about the way He loves us, it truly is hard to fathom, knowing as I do that it is a deeper love than we could ever understand this side of heaven. Yet even if we never come to the fullest comprehension of this love in our lifetimes, He has given us His Word so we can have a taste of just how rich it truly is!

I like to think of the Bible as God's love letter to us, which paints a dynamic picture of all the ways He loves us. My favorite depiction of His love is described in Romans 8:31–38:

What shall we say about such wonderful things as these? If God is for us, who can ever be against us? Since he did not spare even his own Son but gave him up for us all, won't he also give us everything else? Who dares accuse us whom God has chosen for his own? No one—for God himself has given us right standing with himself. Who then will condemn us? No one—for Christ Jesus died for us and was raised to life for us, and he is sitting in the place of honor at God's right hand, pleading for us.

Can anything ever separate us from Christ's love? Does it mean he no longer loves us if we have trouble or calamity, or are persecuted, or hungry, or destitute, or in danger, or threatened with death? (As the Scriptures say, "For your sake we are killed every day; we are being slaughtered like sheep.") No, despite all these things, overwhelming victory is ours through Christ, who loved us.

And I am convinced that nothing can ever separate us from God's love. Neither death nor life, neither angels nor demons, neither our fears for today nor our worries about tomorrow—not even the powers of hell can separate us from God's love.

Just as a good father loves to care for His children, our Heavenly Father longs to care for us, but He will never force us to do anything against our will. In order for Him to get involved in our lives, we need to trust Him as the loving Father He is. Our daily walk with Him makes that possible. The closer we draw to Him, the more we are reminded of how much He loves us, and then it becomes easy to trust in His provision. I believe that as we receive God's love for us, we are able to surrender everything to Him without hesitation, knowing that His plan for us is better than our own.

Jesus invites us to lay our burdens down, saying, "Come to me, all of you who are weary and carry heavy burdens, and I will give you rest" (Matt. 11:28). When we lay our burdens at His feet, He exchanges them for His deep reassuring peace, which brings freedom from the weight we carry. The closer we draw to Him, the more of that freedom we will experience. And in that place we find rest for our souls.

Are you weighed down from carrying heavy burdens or unwanted weight today? Jesus is calling for you to come to Him. He longs for you to trust Him and lay everything down at His feet. As you do, He promises to take the weight of all that you have been carrying and exchange it for His freedom and glorious rest.

FOOD FOR THOUGHT

Nourishment for the Soul

Scripture

Then Jesus said, "Come to me, all of you who are weary and carry heavy burdens, and I will give you rest" (Matt. 11:28).

Reflection Questions

- Did you already believe that God wants you to be free from everything that weighs you down, spiritually, physically, and emotionally, or is this a new truth for you?
- How could a revelation of God's love change the way you carry burdens?
- How can spending time with God help you depend on Him?

Prayer

Dear Lord, I thank You that You, the creator of the universe, care so much about me that You took the time to knit me together in my mother's womb. You created me uniquely and thought about every part of my life before it came to be. I thank You that You love me so deeply that You want to be involved in every area of my life. I pray that You would help me to deepen my walk with You and have a heart revelation of how much You care for me. As I come to an understanding of Your love for me, help me to surrender my need to control and the burdens of everything that weighs me down physically, emotionally, and spiritually. In Jesus' Name, amen.

Nourishment for the Body
Chicken Chickpea Salad

This salad makes a delicious and simple lunch! It is packed with protein, fiber, and healthy fats, making it a perfectly balanced meal that is great to take on the go! It can also be made without the chicken for a fabulous vegetarian meal or side dish.

Ingredients

1 cup diced or shredded
    cooked chicken breast
1 (15.5-ounce) can chickpeas,
    rinsed and drained
1 cup corn
1 cup halved grape tomatoes

¼ cup crumbled feta
½ cup washed and chopped
    fresh cilantro
1 small avocado, diced
1 teaspoon lemon juice

Method

Add all the ingredients to a large bowl and gently toss to combine. Refrigerate until ready to serve.

Yields: 4 servings

3

NOURISHING THE SOUL

So often when we think about health, our thoughts immediately go toward caring for our physical bodies. While it's true that our bodies make up a component of our overall well-being, our health goes well beyond what we can perceive with our five senses.

The truth is, there is more to us than a body that we can touch, see, and feel. In fact, there are two other parts to our triune being, soul and spirit. Our body is often the easiest to identify with out of the three because it is constantly sending us signals based on our physical senses. From the moment we are born, we are accustomed to listening to our bodies' needs as they send us signals that we are hungry, tired, in pain, etc.

The next part of our being is our soul, which is comprised of our mind, will, and emotions. *Our mind* includes our thoughts, attitudes, beliefs, and imaginings. *Our will* is made up of our desires and choices, which ultimately determine our willingness to do something and the outcome of our actions. Last but not least, *our emotions* are an accumulation of feelings derived from our circumstances, relationships, and health.

Many of us find it quite easy to express our will and emotions, and are able to convey exactly what we desire and feel at any given moment. However, many of us are not as in tune with what is going on in our minds. This is because many of us passively allow our thoughts and imaginations to run through our minds without being aware of them. Beyond that, even if we are aware of our thoughts, many of us don't recognize that we have the ability to change them. For that reason a portion of this book will focus solely on reprogramming the way we think, which will in turn improve the health of our souls.

Our final and innermost part is our spirit. When we give our lives to Jesus, the Spirit of God comes to live inside us (see Rom. 8:11). The spirit part of us is also the part that is "born again" when we give our lives to Jesus (see 1 Pet. 1:23). Our spirit is the most important part of our three-part being, as it is the part of us that will inherit eternal salvation when we make Jesus our Lord and Savior.

Healthy from the Inside Out

Over the years I have come to learn that much of our health begins in our souls and then works its way out into our physical bodies. I believe that if we are ever going to experience the fullness of health we so greatly desire, we need to first deal with the health of our souls.

This is often not the way of the world, which typically places a priority on the things we can see. I'm sure we all have stories about how we used every bit of effort to change those things that are visible to the eye.

The good news is that there is a better way. There is hope for not only change, but complete transformation. Beginning this change will be different from what most of us are used to because it begins on the inside. It will still require time and effort on our part, but it will be different from the kind of effort that wears us out.

As I shared in chapter 1, I reached this place of transformation when I made the choice to lay down my own wisdom and will and finally surrender my body to the Lord. The first step I took was going to God and asking for wisdom in caring for my health. To my surprise, God didn't lead me to a nutrition plan, nor did He teach me how to care for my health initially. Instead He led me to Romans 12:2, which revealed His desire to transform me from the inside out.

This life-changing promise reveals that we have a part to play in discovering God's good and perfect will for our lives, which includes His perfect will in caring for our body and soul. Unlike the world's method, however, it won't come through a quick fix or our own effort. Rather, we discover it as we turn away from the patterns of this world and reprogram our minds with the Word of God (see Rom. 12:2).

At the time that God revealed this truth to me, I was specifically searching for God's good, acceptable, and pleasing will for my body. This promise revealed that my transformation would come as I applied its instructions. This meant I would have to stop looking to magazines, diets, and outward solutions when it came to caring for my body, and allow God's Word to reveal my true identity.

How Do You See Yourself?

Almost immediately after God revealed this truth to me, He followed it with a very profound question. As I lay on my bed one day, He whispered to my heart, *Katie, how do you see your-self?* My very next thought was, *What do you mean, Lord? You already know what I think about myself.* His silence told me that I was missing something, and I knew that this question would take some time to answer. So I decided to take a walk, which is one of my favorite ways to calm my heart and hear from the Lord.

I began my walk that day by asking the Lord to reveal the message He was trying to convey to me. The Lord continued to gently probe at my heart, encouraging me to think a little deeper, beyond what I saw in the mirror.

The Holy Spirit began to reveal that the way I was see-ing myself on the inside was what I was ultimately becom-ing on the outside. When I saw myself as having a poor body image and having unhealthy relationships with my body and food, I was ultimately living out the reality of those thought patterns in my daily life. As much as I wanted to break free from these lies, God showed me that change would come only when I renewed my mind and started to see myself through His Word.

I knew from what God had already revealed to me that this would require me to diligently study His Word. Specif-ically, I started to look up Scriptures about my identity and value in Christ, and what He says about my beauty and worth. God also showed me that in order to be transformed holis-tically, I would have to let Him heal the wounds in my soul. This meant that I had to be willing to release the hurts of my past to Him to receive His healing.

He reminded me of His promise in Matthew 6:11, which says, "Give us today the food we need." This Scripture is referring to the nourishment that comes from God's Word. It tells us that just as we need food to fuel our physical bodies, we need God's Word to nourish our souls. He promises that when we partake of His daily bread, it will bring life and health to our souls.

By the time I was done with my walk that day, I was so encouraged and refreshed by what the Lord had revealed to me that I knew I would never be the same. I started to apply the truths of Romans 12:2 to my life, and it was then that I started to see true transformation. I went from a life limited to what I could achieve on my own to one that was free from the frustration and striving of my own effort as I followed God's guidance.

I will admit that this concept was a whole new way of thinking for me, because I had spent so many years trying to control the things I could see. The more I tried to deal with things on a surface level, the more discouraged I became. I finally realized that without a renewed mind and full dependence on God, my life would remain the same, unchanged, no matter how hard I tried to produce change.

The Garden of Our Soul

Learning to care for the health of my soul came full circle for me when I was growing my first vegetable garden. I was so excited about my little garden box. That spring, I planted zucchini, summer squash, bell peppers, tomatoes, and a few different herbs. I now realize I was quite ambitious, since it was my first time gardening, but if nothing else, being overly zealous taught me a powerful lesson.

Daily I ran outside, excited to check on my growing garden, only to realize that there wasn't much growing going on. I came to realize I had to be patient, since it would take quite a few weeks to see any signs of growth, much less any yield! As persistent as I was in checking on the progress of the garden, I somehow missed a very important step in gardening. Within a few weeks, some of the plants were quickly withering and dying.

I was perplexed by what had caused the plants to decline so quickly until I started looking more closely. As I was pulling back some of the leaves, I quickly found the problem. A host of weeds were popping up around my plants, choking the life right out of them. I realized that in the midst of checking on the growth of the plants, I had forgotten to look for anything that didn't belong in the garden, such as weeds, mold, and insects.

I fiercely plucked each and every weed that I could find in my beloved garden, disposing of them like the invaders they were. Within a few days, however, I noticed that the weeds were starting to grow back. As annoying as that was, I took a moment to think about how to solve the problem. It dawned on me that I had to pluck the weeds up by the roots in order to get rid of them for good.

When I began the task of removing the life-sucking weeds from my precious garden, I found it more difficult than I'd originally thought! I was surprised to discover that the roots of these weeds went down deep, often traveling across the bed of soil and entangling themselves with the roots of my vegetables. After I saw this, it became clear to me why the vegetable plants were dying. The roots of the weeds were sucking the life right out of the healthy areas of the garden.

So I used all my strength to dig up and pull out every weed by the root. It was a dirty and hard process, but sure enough, the hard work paid off. Within a few days my plants were springing back to life! From that point forward, I was diligent in checking for any new intruders and maintaining my plants. Eventually they flourished, yielding just as they should. That summer I got an abundance of vegetables and herbs, so many that I was able to give some away!

God used my gardening experience to teach me a powerful lesson. He showed me how our souls (our mind, will, and emotions) can be compared to a garden, and how the way we tend to them will determine how healthy they are (see Isa. 58:11).

This experience painted a clear picture of two different scenarios we can find ourselves in when caring for our souls. The first scenario is comparable to when I first started to tend to the garden, looking only at the growth and health of the plants and neglecting to notice the weeds. God showed me that if we go through life tending only to the good things, but ignore the weeds that are sprouting up, the good things in our lives will eventually be choked out.

The second scenario is comparable to when I took notice of the weeds and broke them off at the tops. Much as I was plucking the weeds at the surface, often we try to change what we can see instead of doing the dirty work and removing the weeds at their roots. When we do this, we will find that it is only a matter of time before the weeds grow back.

I found this to be true in my own life when I tried to control my weight by restricting what I was eating. Regardless of how much weight I lost, I always regained it because I was neglecting the heart of the issue. If, on the other hand, we do the hard work of getting to the root of the problem, we can remove the weed and cut off its ability to survive.

Our souls are much like my garden. As we surrender our lives to Christ and become fully reliant on Him, He becomes our master gardener. He will show us what needs to be uprooted and expose everything that doesn't produce life in our hearts. As we renew our minds, His Word will uproot the lies. When we begin to replace lies with truth, we will finally start to see ourselves through His eyes.

As we progress through this book, we will walk through the steps that lead to the transformation of both body and soul. The first step is to surrender to God and allow His Word to uproot, replant, and nourish our soul, leading to His good, acceptable, and perfect will accomplished in our lives (see Rom. 12:2). And we will begin to flourish just as He designed!

FOOD FOR THOUGHT

Nourishment for the Soul

Scripture

Dear friend, I hope all is well with you and that you are as healthy in body as you are strong in spirit (3 John 1:2).

Reflection Questions

- How do you see yourself on a heart level? (I challenge you to take your time answering this question. Ask God to help you search your heart as you seek to find the answer.)

- Which of the three scenarios do you feel you can most relate to when it comes to dealing with the weeds in your soul? Do you find yourself ignoring the weeds or plucking them off at the surface, or do you take the time to dig them out by the root?

Prayer

Dear Lord, I thank You that You care about the health of my soul, and that it is Your desire and plan for me to be healthy spirit, soul, and body. I pray that You would give me a revelation of Romans 12:2, and that You would empower me to make choices that conform to Your will rather than the pattern of this world. Help me to see myself according to what You say about me in Your Word. Transform me by the renewing of my mind with Your truth. Father, please help me to properly care for the health of my soul, dealing with weeds at a root level and tending to the things that will bear fruit that will last. In Jesus' Name, amen.

Nourishment for the Body
Sweet Potato Turkey Burgers

Have you ever had a turkey burger that was dry and tasteless? These sweet potato turkey burgers are just about guaranteed to revolutionize the way you make and think about turkey burgers! The sweet potato gives the burgers a moist and juicy taste without extra fat and calories. They are wonderful on a whole grain bun, in a lettuce wrap, or simply by themselves.

Ingredients

1 small sweet potato	1 teaspoon salt
1¼ pounds lean ground turkey (or extra-lean ground beef)	¼ teaspoon pepper
	½ teaspoon garlic powder
	½ teaspoon onion powder
½ cup thawed, squeezed dry, and chopped frozen spinach (or 1 cup fresh spinach)	4 whole grain buns or lettuce wraps for serving (optional)

Method

Precook the sweet potato until just tender, but not mushy, by microwaving on high for 4 minutes or baking for 30 minutes in a 375-degree oven. Remove the peel of the sweet potato and break it up with a knife into very small pieces.

Combine the sweet potato, ground turkey, spinach, and seasonings in a large bowl and form the mixture into four patties.

Cook on the grill, pan, or griddle over medium-high heat for about 3 to 4 minutes on each side, or until the burgers are cooked through, or until they reach an internal temperature of 165°F or more.

To serve, place on a bun or lettuce wrap and top with your favorite toppings and condiments.

Yields: 4 servings

4

WHAT'S IN YOUR GARDEN?

*A*ll of this talk about gardens has probably gotten you thinking about the garden of your soul. In fact, you may have even spotted a few weeds that have been robbing you of health for quite some time. If that sounds like you, get your gardening gloves ready!

In this chapter we will be taking an in-depth look at the different types of weeds that can spring up and crowd our soul, as well as how to effectively remove them. This is a vital next step in improving the health of our soul, because in order to make room for a new healthy life, we must first clear out anything that doesn't belong.

I believe you will be encouraged to do some soul searching as you reflect on your past and present and allow the Lord to heal your wounds. This will be incredibly beneficial to the health of your heart and mind, which will in turn make way for optimal health in your body. So let's get to work and dig deep! After all, if we are comparing our soul to a garden, then naturally the next question should be, what's in my garden?

Examining Our Thought Life

As we discussed in the previous chapter, our soul is made up of our mind, will, and emotions. Out of these three areas, I believe it is most crucial to pay attention to what is going on in our mind, because it is our thoughts that ultimately dictate the outcome of our will and emotions. The way we think can cause a cascade effect that ultimately shapes the direction of our lives.

For example, one thought has the ability to formulate a purpose in our heart that is then played out in our actions. Over time our actions become habits, and our habits make up our character; and our character shapes the way we live our lives.

An example of this process starts with volleyball in my elementary school gym class. Every time the ball came toward me I would put up my arms and crouch down to protect myself out of fear that the ball would hit me. Instead of encouraging me or instructing me on how to properly hit the ball, the gym teacher started yelling cruel remarks such as, "You will never be able to play sports if you are scared of a silly ball!"

This event left an impression on me that generated thoughts of inadequacy when it came to sports. Over time those thoughts hindered me from participating in anything sports related, which created a habit of turning down every athletic opportunity that presented itself. It wasn't long until I started to identify myself as "bad at sports." This hindered me from participating in many things throughout my childhood and teen years.

For this reason I don't believe that we will ever be able to move beyond the mental images we have of ourselves if we don't begin to investigate our thought life. For example, if someone has repetitive thoughts of being a failure, they will most likely have a hard time moving beyond how they see themselves on the inside if they never take note of their thoughts. If they don't renew their mind, this thought pattern will eventually be carried out in their life, leading to a pattern of failure.

We will be discussing two different types of weeds in this book, although it is important to note that these aren't the only types that exist. The two that I have chosen to focus on are incredibly common among women I have worked with, and I have dealt with them myself. Before diving in, I encourage you to pray and ask the Lord to reveal any weeds that might be in your heart, whether they're described here or not.

Identifying the Lies We Have Believed

I have come to learn that much of what we see in our lives is the result of a lie that has taken root in the soil of our hearts and minds. For that reason the very first weeds we are going to look for are *lies that we have believed*. To start, we are going to discuss three of the different ways we can receive a lie, which will help us identify them more readily. A lie can come in the form of (1) words, (2) an image, or (3) an experience.

Regardless of the way a lie is received, it is vital that we first recognize the source of all lies. The Devil, who is the "father of lies" (John 8:44), is the source of every lie. Whether those lies come to us through spoken words, images, or experiences, they all go against God's truth and His very nature. The enemy's purpose in forming lies against us is to cause us to doubt our value and worth as a child of God, and ultimately to steal, kill, and destroy anything he can in our lives (see John 10:10). Understanding the common ways we can receive lies, as well as their source, will help us distinguish lies from the truth.

1. Spoken Words

Lies often come into our souls through spoken words, whether through society (media) and culture, others' opinions, or even what we say about ourselves.

Words are incredibly powerful, and they have the ability to create images in our minds and shape how we see ourselves. The Bible also confirms that they have the ability to produce life or death in our lives (see Prov. 18:21). That's powerful!

This was true in my own life when I received the lie that I was overweight from that fourteen-year-old boy in the lunchroom. His cutting words were like a seed that was planted in the depths of my heart. Because I was young and naive, it didn't take long for this lie to take root. Left untouched for so many years, this single weed spread and eventually choked out any remaining life.

Maybe you can relate. Have you ever heard something that planted a lie in your mind? Perhaps someone made a remark about your body, weight, or appearance. Or maybe it was in reference to your personality, abilities, or intelligence. Regardless of the area that was targeted, hurtful words can spread like the weeds they are, polluting the health of our entire soul if left untreated.

Lies can also come to us through our own mouths. Have you ever noticed that this is especially common among women? Why is it that we feel the need to express every negative thought we have about ourselves the moment we get together? Just the other day I was at a restaurant with my husband and overheard a lady next to us tell her friend, "I'm not going to get the cheesecake today. Everyone knows I don't need to add to any cheesiness in my thighs." The two women laughed together and went on with their conversation. As I sat there listening, my heart began to break for that woman.

To some this may sound like harmless venting, or maybe even a lighthearted joke. However, the Bible tells us that our words have the ability to build up and to destroy (see Prov. 13:3). Knowing this to be true, I longed to speak life and truth to that woman, knowing just how dangerous her self-sabotaging words were to the health of her soul.

Some may realize that speaking negative words about ourselves is unhealthy, but what about the times we speak negative words internally? Perhaps you have said to yourself, *You will never lose weight! Why do you even try?* or *Go ahead and eat the whole bag of chips. You've had a hard day. You deserve it!* Whether our words are spoken or not, we must realize that they have the ability to produce either life or death in our lives. It's time to put a guard over our mouths and minds, knowing that our words have the potential to bless or damage our health.

When we are dealing with lies that come in the form of words, not only do we need to uproot these lies, we must also go through the process of releasing any unforgivingness, bitterness, or offense that came with them. This is crucial, because unforgivingness left untreated can form a bitter root that can certainly spoil the health of our garden.

God explains that forgiveness begins when we bless those who curse us, and pray for those who mistreat us (see Luke 6:28). Initially this may seem hard or even impossible, but we can look to Jesus as our example and know that He understands what we are going through. Matthew 27:27–31 paints a detailed picture of how Jesus was mocked and ridiculed before going to the cross. If Jesus was able to forgive and pray for His enemies, then we know we can forgive those who have said hurtful words to us.

As we are obedient in praying for our enemies we invite His grace and love to flow through us, which cover a multitude of sins. His love helps us to see others the way He sees them, making it possible to forgive. This same love also brings life and health to the wounded areas of our soul as we release the person who hurt us and trust Him to be our defender.

2. Images We See

Another way that lies can come to us is through the images we see. These images can come from magazines, billboards, or photographs. No words need be spoken; one quick glimpse of an airbrushed woman on a billboard can produce thoughts telling us that we don't measure up, that we're not as beautiful, not as wanted, not as worthy.

I found this to be true in my own life whenever I flipped through the pages of a fitness or beauty magazine. I used to buy them thinking they were good motivators, yet I noticed they would often leave me feeling more discouraged than inspired. No matter how in shape I was, the images in those magazines left me thinking I needed to lose five to ten pounds and tone up in order to be beautiful.

3. Life Experiences

Last but not least, lies can infiltrate our soul through our daily experiences. Whether we realize it or not, our lives are constantly being influenced by events and interactions. These experiences paint a picture in our minds that then affects the way we view ourselves and the world around us.

Imagine a girl grows up with a domineering father who is critical of her mother's appearance. The young girl may witness her father making critical remarks about her mother's body and scrutinizing her food choices. He may even seem to withhold love and affirmation from her until she looks a certain way. This experience paints a lie in this young girl's mind, telling her she needs to be thin in order to be loved by a man.

Uprooting the Lies by Renewing Our Minds

After we have identified the lies we have believed, we can begin to uproot them. We do this by renewing our mind. In our garden metaphor, this essentially means that we dig up the root of a lie, remove it, and replace it with a truth from God's Word that brings life and health to the garden of our soul. Renewing the mind can be incredibly powerful, because that act has the ability to change our thoughts, attitudes, and actions.

I spent years believing lies that were robbing the health of my soul. It wasn't until I aligned my thoughts and words with what God said about me that my actions began to change. As my old thought patterns were replaced with truth, my health began to return, and I was transformed from the inside out.

The Bible gives us clear instructions on how to renew our minds. Second Corinthians 10:5 instructs us to keep our minds stayed upon the Word of God. If we are diligent to check every word, image, and experience at the door of our minds, we will be able to ask ourselves, "Does this produce thoughts in line with the Word of God?" If the answer is no, then we can be sure that its source is not of God, and therefore that it needs to be dismissed as a lie and replaced with the truth.

Practically speaking, we can renew our mind by reading, studying, meditating on, and praying through God's Word. Regardless of the method, the purpose of renewing our minds is always the same, which is to replace our old thought patterns with the truth of what God says about us.

Meditating on God's Word

One of my favorite ways to renew my mind is through meditating on God's Word. Now, before I lose you, let me clarify that this is unlike the Buddhist practice of meditation. Meditation as it relates to God's Word is the simple practice of aligning our thoughts with His. We can see that this practice is based in Scripture. Joshua found it beneficial, which is why he tells us, "Study this Book of Instruction continually. Meditate on it day and night so you will be sure to obey everything written in it. Only then will you prosper and succeed in all you do" (Josh. 1:8).

You may be thinking, *Who has time for meditation?* Well, whether you realize it or not, we are all meditating on different thoughts daily. Let me give you an example. Have you ever spent your day worrying about something while taking care of your kids, cleaning the house, or doing your job? If so, you have essentially been meditating on something without even realizing it. The only difference between meditating on wrong thoughts (such as our worries, lies, or fears) and meditating on God's promises is that in the latter case we are making the choice to think about what He said.

What I love about the Bible is that it is God's spoken

Word written directly to us. If we want to know His thoughts on a matter, we can find it in the Bible. If we are having a hard time distinguishing a truth from a lie, reading His Word is like turning the light on in a dark room. At last you can see things for what they really are. Lastly, the Bible is God breathed, which means that it is filled with promises that are brought to life by the power of His Spirit. And when God makes a promise, He can never take it back!

I've mentioned that one of the ways I like to renew my mind is by listening to sermons on my iPod. We have such an advantage in today's society, with all the podcasts, sermons, and audio Bibles at our fingertips. In fact, we have so many resources that there is really no excuse not to spend time in the Word of God!

We can also meditate on God's Word by keeping it before our eyes. Personally, I like to do this by writing out on note-cards Scriptures that pertain to whatever I may be going through in a given season. I tape them up everywhere I can see them—on my mirror, on my fridge, in my car, etc.—and this reminds me to purposefully think on those things that are pure, just, right, holy, and of a good report (see Phil. 4:8). These notes are great reminders to keep my thoughts in check, which can be especially important on busy or emotional days.

Praying God's Word

When I was in the midst of my battle with eating disorders, I knew it would require a fight to break free. When I began to fight for my health, I knew I would gain the victory if I used the weapons He gave me. God explains that the weapons He has given us are spiritual in nature, and they are strong and mighty to overcome strongholds (see 2 Cor. 10:4). Many of these weapons are for defending ourselves against the schemes of the enemy, but one is specifically used to fight offensively against our adversary. This weapon is the Word of God, which is referred to as the sword of the Spirit (see Eph. 6:17).

Not only is the spoken Word of God a mighty weapon to overcome strongholds, it is also powerful in the everyday battles going on in our minds. If we allow the lies that come at us to enter untouched, eventually these lies will grow, and every area of our soul (and even our body) will be affected. But a mind defended with God's Word has the power to be renewed until it conforms to the image of Christ.

When we have daily battles in our minds, or are facing temptations, we sometimes think we should pray and ask God to take these thoughts or temptations away. Yet if we look at Jesus and how He responded when He was lied to and tempted, we can see that He didn't pray and ask God to deliver Him. Interestingly, when Jesus was being tempted in the wilderness, we saw Him using the Word of God as an offensive weapon in the midst of his spiritual battle (see Matt. 4:1–11). If Jesus is our example, we know we should respond to the battles in our mind in the same way.

How Do We Pray God's Word?

Renewing our mind by praying God's Word begins with spending time with Jesus. (Are you beginning to see how fellowship with the Lord is the foundation of our freedom?) As we read the Bible, we can ask the Holy Spirit to guide us to Scriptures that apply to our specific situation. Begin to look at the areas of your life (or mind) that need to be covered in prayer, and pick the weapon specifically designed for the battle you are facing.

One effective way I found to do this is to create a lies versus truth chart. On the left side I wrote down all the areas where I had believed a lie. On the right side I wrote down truths from God's Word that refuted those lies. (See the appendix at the back of the book for an example.) I then created Scripture-based prayers from the truths I'd written down, knowing that they were the precise weapons I needed to combat the lies I was believing. (Take note, this is just one way I personally began writing Scripture-based prayers; it certainly isn't necessary that you make a chart every time.)

To write out a Scripture-based prayer, simply take the truths that you find in God's Word and apply them to your situation. Oftentimes this is as simple as writing down a Scripture and applying your name to claim possession of the promise. (Remember, God wrote these promises to you and for you in the first place! You can also use someone else's name if you are looking to cover someone else in prayer.) In addition to fighting off the lies of the enemy, praying God's Word is a powerful way of reminding ourselves what God said about us and assuring our hearts of His promises.

The Prayer of Faith

When we pray according to the Word, we can do so with faith and boldness, knowing that we are praying in line with His will (because His Word and will are always in agreement). We also have a promise to confirm this truth in 1 John. Here the disciple John tells us, "This is the confidence which we have before Him, that, if we ask anything according to His will, He hears us. And if we know that He hears us *in* whatever we ask, we know that we have the requests which we have asked from Him" (v. 5:14–15 NASB). This promise gives me assurance that whatever I am praying for in in accordance with His Word will come to pass in His perfect timing.

All throughout Scripture we can see examples of different men and women who received a promise because they prayed in faith and knew God was faithful to His Word. We can see this clearly when looking at Abraham. God gave him a promise that he would become the father of many nations when his wife was well past the age to bear children (they were both about a hundred years of age). Abraham had no reason in the natural to believe God, and to be quite honest, if he looked at his circumstances, he surely had reason to doubt.

Yet Abraham didn't let his circumstances sway him. He ended up receiving the promise because he knew God would be faithful in bringing His Word to pass. The Bible tells us that this type of faith brought glory to God, and that because of it Abraham was counted as righteous (see Rom. 4:20–21).

Just like Abraham, we can have full assurance that God is faithful to His promises. No matter what we see going on around us, we must have full assurance that He is able to do what He said in His Word.

Identifying the Cares That Burden Us

Once we start to plant the truth of God's Word, we need to protect our hearts against another type of weed: the cares of this life. The Bible specifically warns us to be on guard against them. Mark 4:19 compares the cares of this life to weeds that have the potential to enter in and choke the Word of God that we have planted in our hearts. For that reason we must be vigilant in removing the cares in our lives as quickly as they spring up.

Cares can come to us in different forms, but the most common are anxiety, worry, and stress. Oftentimes these cares come to us as a result of pressures that arise in our finances, relationships, work, or family, or from living an overly busy, unbalanced lifestyle.

Stress in particular can take a toll on the health of our soul, as it affects our emotions, thoughts, and behavior. This translates into the health of our bodies as well, leaving us with physical ramifications such as tension headaches, stomach-aches, high blood pressure, and chronic illness, just to name a few. Although at times we would like to believe that we are superhumans, holding on to worries, cares, and stress will always eventually take a toll on our entire being.

Martha and Mary

When I think about being burdened by the cares of this life, I am reminded of the story of Martha and Mary in the Bible (see Luke 10:38–42). In this passage Martha is busy trying to be a good hostess to her guest, Jesus. While she is busy serving, her sister Mary is resting at Jesus' feet, listening to what He has to say.

After a while Martha becomes agitated because she is doing all the work, so she asks Jesus, "'Lord, doesn't it seem unfair to you that my sister just sits here while I do all the work? Tell her to come and help me'" (v. 40). Jesus answers her, "But the Lord said to her, 'My dear Martha, you are worried and upset over all these details! There is only one thing worth being concerned about. Mary has discovered it, and it will not be taken away from her'" (v. 41–42).

Two things are happening in this passage. First, it reveals the heart motive of these two sisters. It's clear that Martha's primary concern is to be a proper hostess, while Mary's focus is on being a disciple of Jesus. Second, we can see from Jesus' response how He feels about both of these women's motives. Although He doesn't negate Martha's hospitality, He is concerned with the fact that she is distracted and troubled by her serving. Although her intentions are good, they ultimately take her attention off the one thing that matters most: Jesus.

I wonder how many of us can relate to being the Martha in this story? I know I sure can! Being a woman in today's society places many demands on our time, attention, and heart. If we aren't busy tending to our home and family, we are most likely working in a career or serving our community or church. All of these factors place an extraordinary amount of pressure on us, and we can become overwhelmed with the cares of this life.

Unfortunately, these cares can easily be written off as normal, making them difficult to distinguish and remove. In our culture, being stressed is often viewed as a glorified form of being busy. While it is beneficial to be productive, there is something to be said for finding a healthy balance and setting boundaries.

I learned this personally about two years ago. I was in a state of extreme emotional stress at the time because I was so busy with Dashing Dish, being a good wife, caring for our home, and writing two books at the same time. Although everything I was doing was "good" and most of it was ministry in some form or other, I took on too much at once. My priorities got out of balance, and eventually any time for rest (including my daily quiet time with the Lord) suffered.

Eventually the weight of everything came crashing down around me, taking a toll on me mentally, emotionally, and physically. I started to get worn out by simple tasks, I was more irritable, and I felt burned out overall. Women especially can get so busy doing "good" things that their hearts become troubled, distracting them from what matters most. After that experience I can say with assurance that we need to deal with stress, anxiety, and worry before we can come to a place of health in body and soul.

Uprooting the Cares

This brings us to our next question: how do we uproot the cares in the garden of our soul? The first step is to fully surrender every area that concerns us to the Lord. When we do this, it not only releases us from the burdens we were never intended to carry, it also prevents us from developing the behaviors and mind-sets that go along with an unhealthy desire to control.

For me, this desire for control came in the form of eating disorders. They were my attempt to cope with intense emotions that were not surrendered to the Lord. For a time, being in control of my weight gave me the illusion that I was truly in control in the midst of my chaos. Now, looking back, I see how out of control my life really was!

Releasing Our Cares through Prayer

One of the ways we can surrender our cares to the Lord is by releasing them to God through continual prayer. Philippians 4:6 instructs us to do this very thing: "Don't worry about anything; instead, pray about everything. Tell God what you need, and thank him for all he has done." I love this promise, because it reminds us that we can come to Jesus with everything that weighs on our hearts, surrendering all to Him. As we entrust our cares to Christ instead of fretting over them, we transfer the heavy burden of our soul into God's hands. And He always makes good on the promise.

This passage goes on to say that when you surrender your cares and trust Him, "Then you will experience God's peace, which exceeds anything we can understand. His peace will guard your hearts and minds as you live in Christ Jesus" (Philippians 4:7). Prayer and peace are closely connected. When we thank Him for all He has done, we are confirming our trust in His ability to take care of us. In exchange for our burdens, He promises to give us His perfect peace.

Prayer in itself is a beautiful act of humility because we are acknowledging God as powerful enough to handle our situation. Every time we cast our cares on the Lord, we are admitting that we are not able to do things on our own, which helps us make the shift from relying on ourselves to relying on God. I also find that as we come to Him in prayer, our awareness of

His greatness and love toward us becomes a habit, helping us depend on Him more and more.

Personally, I like to pray Scripture-based prayers when I am feeling burdened, because it reminds me of Who God really is, and what He said. Then I am able to pray with assurance. When we pray in faith, we can expect that Jesus, our Shepherd, will provide as we release care over to Him. We can rest, knowing that He will refresh, comfort, nourish, and protect us.

I believe that prayers prayed in faith are not only powerful, but also please the Lord. I think of how it must bless His heart when we trust Him as Father! I can almost picture Him running to our aid the moment we call on Him, ready to lift the burdens we lay at His feet.

Release Our Cares through Journaling

Another way I like to take my cares to the Lord is through journaling. First thing in the morning I journal, often taking a few minutes to write down anything that is on my heart, as well as different Scriptures pertaining to my situation. Writing down my thoughts often allows me to clear my head, as well as allowing me to freely express my thoughts to the Lord. When I see the Scriptures written next to the very things that concern me, I am reminded of His goodness and thank Him for His promises to care for me.

I also love to journal because it allows me to look back and see the faithfulness of God! Looking back and remembering is so important. It assures our hearts—if He has done it once, He can do it again!

Continually Casting Our Cares

I don't believe that entrusting our cares to the Lord is a one-time event, any more than renewing our mind is. Rather, it is a choice we need to make daily. When we notice the cares of this life starting to spring up, we know we need to take a moment and prayerfully release them back to our Heavenly Father.

If we have already prayed and given an area of our lives over to the Lord but find ourselves still worrying about it, it is most likely because we have tried to take control of that thing once again. In this case the solution is simple. We need to recognize that He has promised to take care of us, guide us, and provide for us. If we find ourselves worrying about something again, we should stop those thoughts in their tracks and say, "No, I refuse to worry about this thing anymore, because God is taking care of it!" Release it once and for all over to Him.

What's in Your Garden?

When it comes to the health of our soul, we will never be able to receive the life-giving nourishment that comes from God and His Word if we don't first deal with the things that could potentially choke it out.

The Bible encourages us to think on those things that are true, noble, right, pure, lovely, admirable, and excellent or worthy of praise (see Phil. 4:8). This is essentially the tool by which we can measure the health of our soul. As we look through our garden and find things that are not producing life, we can almost always trace them back to a lie we have believed, a care we have been burdened by, or another type of weed that has choked out the truth.

Although we live in a world that bombards us with lies, cares, and messages that are contrary to the truth, God has given us every tool we need to uproot those things that don't belong. This regular upkeep produces health in our mind, will, and emotions, which carries over to the health of our physical body. It will take time and diligence, but if we want a healthy body and soul, we must ask ourselves regularly, what's in my garden?

FOOD FOR THOUGHT

Nourishment for the Soul

Scripture

Give your burdens to the LORD, and he will take care of you. He will not permit the godly to slip and fall (Ps. 55:22).

Reflection Questions

- Have you ever taken the time to account for what's going on in the garden of your soul? If not, how do you plan to begin doing so?
- Have you ever received lies about yourself based on words, images you came across, or experiences in your life? How can you begin to uproot these lies and replace them with truth?
- Do you find yourself regularly taking on the cares of this life? How can you begin to deal in a productive way with the things that trouble your mind?

Prayer

Dear Lord, I ask that You would examine my heart and mind and reveal any thoughts that are contrary to Your truth. Please uproot any thoughts that are counterproductive to Your Word, and give me an awareness of when these thoughts try to creep back in. Help me to recognize any lie of the enemy and to replace those lies with the truth of Your Word. When I am tempted to be worried, please remind me that You go before me and are always with me. Thank You that You never forsake those who seek You. As I surrender my burdens and cares to You, teach me to confidently trust in You. Strengthen my faith so I will not be afraid of what the future holds or discouraged by my circumstances. I hold on to Your promise that as I seek first Your Kingdom, You will provide all I need. I thank You for caring for me, Father! In Jesus' Name, amen.

Nourishment for the Body
Healthier Chocolate Chip Oatmeal Cookies

These chocolate chip oatmeal cookies are refined-flour free, and they don't contain any oil, butter, or white flour. They taste so close to the traditional version that you won't even know they are better for you. Now you can have your cookie and eat it too!

Ingredients

Nonstick cooking spray
¼ cup dark chocolate chips

Dry

¾ cup oat flour (old-fashioned oats blended into a flour)

¾ cup old-fashioned oats

¾ teaspoon baking soda

1 teaspoon cinnamon

½ cup baking stevia (or 1 cup sweetener that measures like sugar)

⅛ teaspoon salt

Wet

1 teaspoon vanilla extract

1 large egg

½ cup peanut butter (or nut butter of choice)

2 tablespoons honey

Method

Preheat oven to 350°F. Line a cookie sheet with parchment paper or foil sprayed with nonstick cooking spray.

Add the dry ingredients to a medium bowl and stir to combine. In a separate medium bowl, combined wet ingredients and stir to combine. Add the wet ingredients to the dry ingredients and stir until mixture forms a dough. Stir in chocolate chips.

Separate dough into 10 balls. Flatten each ball into a cookie-shaped disk. Place cookies on prepared pan. Bake 7 to 8 minutes or until cookies are just set. Remove from oven and let cool.

Yields: 10 cookies

5

BEARING FRUIT THAT WILL LAST

*E*ven if your experience with gardening is minimal (or nonexistent), we all know that a healthy garden requires more than the occasional weeding. In order for a garden to produce fruit of any kind, it is equally important to cultivate and nurture what we want to grow. I believe we are able to accurately gauge the health of our soul by the fruit being produced. After all, a healthy garden yields healthy fruit.

As followers of Jesus, we should aim to produce fruit that will last (see John 15:16). In order for us to accomplish this, we need to be diligent in caring for the life-giving fruit of the spirit that God produces in our lives: "love, joy, peace, patience, kindness, goodness, faithfulness, gentleness, and self-control" (Gal. 5:22–23). As these fruits grow, they will affect our lives (and the lives of those around us), shaping our thoughts, attitudes, and characters, ultimately affecting our actions and overall well-being.

The good news is that these fruits are not something we have to produce ourselves. Rather, they are given to us as a gift from our Heavenly Father. When we accept Jesus as our Savior, God's Holy Spirit comes to live inside us (see 1 Cor. 3:16). With Him, He brings the Fruits of the Spirit, which we receive in seed form. Growing these seeds into mature fruits creates the foundation for a healthy soul, which translates into a healthy, balanced life—mentally, emotionally, and physically.

Staying Connected to the Vine

If we already have these fruit-producing seeds on the inside, how do we care for them so that they grow and mature properly? Just as we don't have to produce the fruit, the growth process isn't something that we have to accomplish in our own strength—in fact, we couldn't, even if we tried. The Holy Spirit comes alongside us and causes the growth to occur in our lives. The only difference is that the growth requires action on our part.

Jesus explains our part in John 15:4, where He says, "Remain in me, and I will remain in you. For a branch cannot produce fruit if it is severed from the vine, and you cannot be fruitful unless you remain in me." This passage tells us that the amount of fruit we produce directly correlates to how closely we abide in Him and obey His commands. How, then, do we abide in Christ in order to produce the fruit we so greatly desire? I am going to discuss three different ways.

First, abiding with Christ means abiding in the Word of God. As we have already learned, when we allow His Word to fill our lives, it will transform our mind, will, and emotions, and these will then direct the desires of our hearts. This truth is clearly portrayed in Psalm 1:

> Blessed is the man
> that walks not in the counsel of the ungodly,
> nor stands in the way of sinners,
> nor sits in the seat of the scornful.
> But his delight is in the law of the LORD;
> and in His law does he meditate day and night.

And he shall be like a tree planted by the rivers of
water,
> that brings forth his fruit in his season;
> his leaf also shall not wither;
> and whatsoever he does shall prosper. (Psalm 1:1–3)

This passage clearly demonstrates how abiding in God's
Word puts our hearts in union with His. As we stay connected
to His Word, we remain connected to the Vine, receiving the
life-giving nourishment that comes from Him.

**Second, Jesus tells us that in order to abide in Him we
must "abide in his love."** He goes on to say that in order to
abide in His love, we must be obedient to His command-
ments (see John 15:9–10). This love was demonstrated to us by
the ultimate act of obedience when Christ went to the cross.
Walking in His kind of love requires us to walk in obedience
to His will with a joyful attitude. Obedience will also require
us to make sacrifices and choices that don't always please the
flesh (more on this later), but it will always produce fruit, and
it is always for our good.

**Finally, union with Christ means submitting to the
pruning process.** Jesus tells us that he prunes the branches
that bear fruit so they will produce even more (see John
15:2). In the natural, when a plant is pruned, the branches
that are dead, damaged, and diseased are cut away in order
to provide life to those branches that bear fruit. This encourages the plant to thrive. As the Vinedresser prunes what
doesn't belong, the energy that was being wasted on distractions is then directed toward producing fruit. In the same way,
when we are pruned of anger, unforgiveness, bitterness, and

negativity, our strength will be restored and we will become more effective at what He is calling us to do.

The result of abiding in Christ is the growth of mature fruit, but we must recognize that it will require patience. Just as a fruit tree takes time to produce fruit, we must also realize that it takes time for God's life-giving nourishment to bring forth fruit that will last. As I mentioned, I was a bit impatient when it came to my first vegetable garden. I would go out and check on the growth of the plants almost every day, as if they were going to shoot up overnight. This led to frustration and disappointment. Then one day I realized that almost everything good in life takes time. When diligence and patience are working together, we will produce fruit that lasts.

Mature Fruit Provides Nourishment

How does all of this apply to our health? We live in a world where we are tempted with self-centeredness and self-reliance every single day. Abiding in Christ brings us to a place of humility, where we acknowledge that we cannot do anything apart from Him. In turn the Holy Spirit goes to work in our lives, developing the Fruits of the Spirit in us. As we produce fruit, it will affect every part of our being, including the health of our body and soul.

When it comes to the health of our bodies, for example, if you find that you struggle with unhealthy behaviors (such as overeating), the fruit of self-control will help you resist temptation and put down your fork once you have had enough. If patience is something you struggle with in your soul, you will find that it can be produced without striving when the fruit of patience is developed in you.

Maintaining Our Gardens

It can be incredibly exciting to see your garden start to flourish, where things that were once withering and dead come alive and start to thrive! When this happens, we can certainly celebrate, although we must be careful not to go on autopilot and stop tending to our garden. Much as we would continue to care for a garden even after it started to flourish, we must continue to carefully guard the health of our soul.

The Bible often refers to our soul as our heart. Proverbs 4:23 confirms that paying attention to what's coming into our heart is vital: "Guard your heart above all else, for it determines the course of your life." This Scripture tells us that this one action (guarding our heart), has the power to change the direction of our entire life. I don't know about you, but when I see a cause credited with an effect of this magnitude in God's Word, it grabs my attention.

So how do we put a guard on our heart? First, we must protect our heart in those areas from the weeds that have grown in our hearts previously. If we look at the weeds we discussed in the previous chapter, we can see that two of these weeds are the cares of this life as well as the lies we have believed. Vulnerable areas can also include anything else that would pollute the health of our soul, such as bitterness, jealousy, and anger, just to name a few.

Guarding Our Hearts against the Lies We Have Believed

One of the best ways to guard our heart against lies we have believed is by taking an inventory of what is coming into our hearts. We can do this by evaluating things we are reading, listening to, and looking at, and ways we are spending our time. We can then ask ourselves, is this drawing my heart closer to God or to this world?

The areas I typically look at are those that have the ability to affect my thought life as it relates to my body image. For example, I found it incredibly helpful in guarding my heart against the pressures of achieving a "perfect" appearance when I stopped reading fashion and health magazines. I also stopped watching certain shows that encourage unhealthy eating patterns or unrealistic standards for women.

Ultimately, we can determine if something is harmful or beneficial to the health of our heart by assessing the thoughts it is producing in us. Whether we're considering something that we are listening to or looking at, we need to be honest and ask ourselves if these things are producing thoughts that align with God's Word. We can also judge our thoughts more accurately by measuring them against Philippians 4:8, as we discussed in chapter 4. Dwelling on those things that are pure, just, right, holy, and of a good report will keep our minds in line with the truth and build a guard around our hearts.

Another way we can guard our hearts is by asking God to reveal anything in our lives that isn't life giving. His wisdom and guidance will prevent us from evaluating things on our own, such as a show we like to watch or the amount of time we spend on social media. These things can seem innocent, yet they can be very dangerous to our hearts. I believe we do ourselves a huge disservice when we try to figure things out on our own and don't partake of God's wisdom.

For example, years ago I knew there were things in my life

that weren't a good influence on my heart, yet I wasn't willing to give them up right away. I was spending too much time on social media, reading fitness magazines, and watching television shows. For a while I made excuses for doing these things, and to be honest, they didn't "seem" that bad. That is, until I asked the Lord to reveal anything that was polluting the health of my heart. When He confirmed the very things I already knew deep down, I was quick to heed His correction, knowing that it had the ability to affect the course of my life. Looking back, it was difficult to give up those things, but I now know that act protected me from needless heartache.

When it comes to guarding your heart, I encourage you to ask yourself, What has the potential to expose my heart to the lies I have worked so hard to uproot? This may require you to be selective about the entertainment you enjoy, how you spend time on the Internet, or whom you spend your time with. Have confidence, knowing that guarding the wellspring of your life is worth anything you give up or limit your exposure to.

Guarding Our Hearts against the Cares of This Life

Likewise, when it comes to guarding your heart against the cares of this life, I would encourage you to take an inventory of the things that are causing you to have worry, stress, and anxiety. If you are feeling stressed out, perhaps you need to reestablish your priorities and set up healthy boundaries. If financial pressures are overwhelming your heart, it may be beneficial to sit down and work on a budget.

I have learned to apply the principles of guarding my heart in my own life after living in a state of constant stress for many years. I was finally forced to change my ways after realizing how badly stress was affecting my health. I started by taking a look at the things that were occupying my time and made a list of the things that weren't necessarily priorities. I decided to cut anything out that was stealing my time, energy, and peace of mind.

In addition, I made the decision to establish a time for work and a time for rest each day. Contrary to what I'd previously believed, I realized that I was actually more productive when I took the evenings and weekends off to enjoy time with friends and family. Managing my time lowered my stress and brought me closer to the Lord because it caused me to depend on Him in a greater way.

Since that initial decision, I now make all my decisions regarding time management according to Psalm 34:14, which instructs us to "seek peace and pursue it." When an opportunity presents itself, I consider the time and energy it will require, and then I pray for wisdom. I ask myself, "Does the thought of this opportunity bring me peace?" If the answer is no, then I respectfully decline, regardless of how good the opportunity may be. I believe this is a biblical and wise way of budgeting and investing the time we have been given.

When it comes to guarding your heart against the cares of this life, I would encourage you to ask yourself, What has the potential of exposing your heart to anxiety, worry, and stress? You may be as I was and have a problem with overworking and need to learn to budget your time. Or maybe you have a tendency to worry about things that you can't control, and you need to lay them at the feet of Jesus. Taking an inventory of the things weighing on you will equip you to make the changes necessary to guard your heart and remain at peace.

FOOD FOR THOUGHT

Nourishment for the Soul

Scripture

"But blessed are those who trust in the LORD and have made the LORD their hope and confidence. They are like trees planted along a riverbank, with roots that reach deep into the water. Such trees are not bothered by the heat or worried by long months of drought. Their leaves stay green, and they never stop producing fruit" (Jer. 17:7–8).

Reflection Questions

- As a follower of Jesus, how do you grow and develop the Fruits of the Spirit inside yourself?
- What are three ways one can abide in Christ? How can you apply them to your own life?
- What does guarding your heart look like to you? How can you guard your heart against the lies and cares of this world?
- How does bearing fruit affect the health of your body and soul?

Prayer

Dear Lord, Your Word says that You are the Vine, which is the source of nourishment and life. Help me to recognize that in order to produce fruit, I must remain in You. Help me to learn what it means to abide in You, Your Word, and

Your love daily so that I will bear much fruit. I pray that You, the great gardener, will cut off any branch in me that does not produce fruit, and that You will prune the branches in me that do bear fruit, so they will produce even more. Help me to pay attention to what I am listening to and looking at, and help me to guard my heart against anything that would infiltrate my mind in a negative way. Instead help me to seek out what is pleasing to You and edifying to my soul. May my hope in You bring peace and strength in my spirit, soul, and body today. In Jesus' Name, amen.

Nourishment for the Body
Make-Ahead Freezer Smoothie Packs

These smoothie packs are the perfect breakfast option for a busy morning! Simply put them together ahead of time, and when you're ready to use one, blend up all the ingredients with almond milk or another milk of your choice. Now you have a delicious, nutritious, perfectly balanced breakfast!

Ingredients

2 cups plain low-fat Greek yogurt

2 to 4 tablespoons stevia or sweetener of choice (or to taste)

2 large bananas, sliced into disks (or other fruit of choice)

4 cups frozen strawberries (or other berries of choice)

4 cups unsweetened almond milk (or other low-fat milk of choice)

Method

Mix yogurt and sweetener in a small bowl and spread evenly into an ice cube tray. Freeze yogurt for at least 4 hours or until frozen.

Once the yogurt is frozen, begin making your smoothie packs. Start by placing half a banana and 1 cup of berries into a freezer bag, along with four frozen yogurt cubes. Seal each bag and place into freezer until ready to use.

To make a smoothie, add 1 cup milk to a blender, followed by the ingredients for one of the smoothie packs. Blend until smooth.

Yields: 4 servings

6
STRENGTHENING YOUR SPIRITUAL MUSCLES

*N*ow that we have talked about how to care for the health of our soul, let's talk about how all of this relates to caring for our physical body. Because, let's face it: we still need to know how to say no to eating an entire plate of cookies! We spent most of the previous chapters talking about how renewing our mind helps improve the health of our soul, so in this chapter we will be talking about how doing so can help us care for our physical body.

The Bible tells us in Ephesians 4:22–24 that when we renew our minds, we are empowered to say no to our old sinful nature and walk by the Spirit of God. The Scripture says, "Put off your old self, which is being corrupted by its deceitful desires; to be made new in the attitude of your minds; and... put on the new self, created to be like God in true righteousness and holiness" (NIV).

This passage tells us that the battles we contend with in the flesh (such as our battle with the cookies) come down to a simple choice. We could respond according to the flesh (our old sinful nature), or we could allow the Spirit of God to renew our thoughts and attitudes, and respond according to our new nature. The term "old self" in this passage is referring to our flesh, or our sinful nature...but I like to think of our "flesh" as an untrained two-year-old!

Our Tantrum-Throwing Flesh

Picture with me for a moment: You are walking down the aisle of a store. It's your day off, you're by yourself, and you actually have some leisure time to shop! You might even stop to grab a cup of Starbucks to enjoy along the way. As you are sipping your coffee with a grin on your face, enjoying the rare quiet time by yourself, you suddenly hear a loud shriek. You jump from the shock, spilling your coffee, and immediately lose your smile. You get to the end of the aisle and peer over to see where the noise came from. A two-year-old is on the ground throwing a temper tantrum. It doesn't take long for you to identify the cause of this tempter tantrum...Can you guess what it was? Yes, that's right, the child didn't get the toy she wanted! You try not to stare as you walk on, your heart going out to the mom who has to deal with the tantruming child.

We have all witnessed a scene like this, a classic two-year-old temper tantrum. When we see a child throwing a tantrum in public, we often feel a bit alarmed by the behavior, yet we understand that the child is young, and hasn't yet learned how to behave properly. Now, imagine for a moment what it would look like if we witnessed these same behaviors coming from an adult! I can just about guarantee that our reaction would go from alarmed to downright appalled! Yet, if we were to be honest with ourselves, how many of us act like this untrained child in at least one area of our lives?

Going back to that plate of cookies, how many of us have ever made the choice to eat one single cookie, only to find that just as we start to walk away, that plate of freshly baked cookies begins to call our name, begging us to have just one more? We try to resist in our minds, telling ourselves that we didn't want to eat more than one, yet something in our flesh begins to cry out, almost as if it is screaming and throwing a fit until it gets its way! Moments later, we find ourselves running back to the very thing that we told ourselves we were done with, and before we know it we have devoured two, three, or even a dozen more cookies than we planned.

When we give in to our every desire without restraint, we are essentially acting like that child who is throwing a temper tantrum until she gets her way. Although it may seem like a good idea to give in to the flesh at the time, it often leads to feelings of guilt and shame, and robs us of our peace later on. Romans 8:6 tells us that "letting your sinful nature [flesh] control your mind leads to death. But letting the Spirit control your mind leads to life and peace." This Scripture confirms to us that it doesn't matter how good something seems. If it is contrary to the wisdom or the Word of God, it will ultimately bring sorrow in our lives.

If we follow the flesh, giving in to every desire much like that unrestrained child, there will be consequences. Whether it is the death of our peace and joy, or even the destruction of our health, there will always be a negative outcome when we give in to our flesh. On the other hand, if we choose to be led by the Spirit of God, then we will reap the benefits of life and peace. I don't know about you, but I would much rather live a life of peace than one of destruction.

Being Led by the Spirit of God

Learning to walk by the Spirit is a vital part of living a healthy lifestyle. When it comes to caring for our physical bodies, so often the flesh will tell us, "Eating this will make you happy" or "You really deserve this doughnut." In moments when we are feeling the flesh pull us to make an unhealthy decision, the Spirit of God can provide everything we need to break the power of temptation.

How, then, are we led by the Spirit of God? The first thing we need to do is be sure that we are a born-again Christian. If you believe and trust in Christ as your Lord, then you are born again and have the Holy Spirit within you. It is the Holy Spirit Who enables us to live a life of holiness and walk in the freedom that Jesus provided for us. If we want to make lasting changes in any area of our life, it crucial that we learn to rely on the Holy Spirit's power and not just our own efforts. When we involve the Holy Spirit in our daily lives and rely on His guidance, He gives us the strength to make the right decisions.

The next thing we need to do is learn how to recognize the Holy Spirit's leading. If we can't distinguish between the leading of our flesh and the leading of the Holy Spirit, it will be hard to discern what we are to follow. Personally, I find it easiest to determine if the Spirit is leading me by reflecting on how I am thinking, acting, and feeling. If my thoughts, behavior, and feelings line up with the Word of God, I know that the born-again part of me is responding to God's Spirit (because we know that God's Spirit will always agree with

God's Word). If, however, my attitudes and actions are sinful, I know I am being led by what the Bible refers to as the "works of the flesh." Galatians 5:19–21 tells us that these "works of the flesh" (KJV) include sexual immorality, impurity, sensuality, idolatry, outbursts of anger, disputes, dissensions, factions, envying, drunkenness, carousing, and anything that takes the place of trusting in the Lord.

Three Keys to Walking by the Spirit

Once we have a clear understanding of what it means to be led by the Spirit, we can begin to walk it out! There are three keys to being led by the Spirit: *repentance*, *prayer*, and *renewing our mind*.

Repentance

The first step is repentance. To repent means to do a complete turnaround or change of direction in our walk with God. When we first give our heart and life to Christ, we are making the choice to turn from our sinful nature and surrender everything to Him. It doesn't end there, however, because our relationship with Christ is a lifetime journey and a continual decision.

After we are born again, we still have to contend regularly with our old sinful nature and selfish tendencies. Continuing in a lifestyle of repentance looks a bit different from first coming to Christ, because we are now in a right-standing position with Him. Instead of repentance making us a new creation, it is now a way for us to get honest with God as we bring our failures and weaknesses to Him. This keeps our hearts sensitive to Him so that He is able to continue the good work He has begun in us. Most important, repentance keeps us in a place of full surrender and submission to the Spirit of God, which is essential to being led by His Spirit.

Prayer

Prayer is the second key to being led by the Spirit of God. As we communicate with the Lord throughout the day, He will give us understanding, discernment, and wisdom, as well as the very power to overcome sin. It is so important that we make time to spend with the Lord each day, communing with Him and drawing on His strength and wisdom.

If we look at Jesus, Who was without sin, we can see that He took time to escape from the crowds each day and spend time in prayer with the Father. If Jesus used prayer as a means to overcome temptation, we would be wise to follow His example! In fact, Jesus instructs us to do the same. Matthew 26:41 tells us, "'Keep watch and pray, so that you will not give in to temptation. For the spirit is willing, but the body is weak.'"

God has given us various types of prayer in order to overcome spiritual battles. The Bible tells us that we are to be "praying at all times in the Spirit, with all prayer and supplication" (Eph. 6:18). In addition to the ability to pray in the Spirit, God has given us the prayer of faith, the prayer of intercession, the prayer of consecration, and the prayer of agreement. If you aren't familiar with each of these types of prayer, I would encourage you to seek them out in the Scriptures and take advantage of all that is available to you as a child of God.

God's Word and His Spirit

Finally, renewing our minds with God's Word is key to being led by the Spirit, because it causes us to be changed from our old nature to our new nature. When we are born again, we still have old habits, thoughts, and behaviors that need to be renewed. As we spend time in God's Word and in His presence, we are transformed from the inside out, conforming to the image of His Son.

Studying God's Word also guards us from giving in to the temptation of our sinful nature. David makes reference to this in Psalm 119:11 when he says, "I have hidden your word in my heart that I might not sin against you" (NIV). When we do our part and faithfully deposit God's Word into our hearts, the Holy Spirit will bring what we have learned to our remembrance, equipping us better to discern that which is good and that which is evil (see John 14:26).

We can see that even Jesus Himself, who was tempted in every way, yet was without sin, used God's Word to overcome temptation (see Heb. 4:15). After Jesus was baptized in the Holy Spirit, He was tempted in the desert by Satan (see Matt. 3–4). When He was being tempted, He drew upon the power of God's Spirit within Him and the Word of God that was stored in His heart to resist the enemy. Likewise, when we rely on the strength of God's Spirit within us and store God's Word in our hearts, we will have everything we need to resist temptation.

As we store God's Word in our hearts, the Spirit of God is able to draw it up for us to use when we need it. Often we won't have time to open our Bible and find a Scripture that applies to our situation. When God's promises are stored in your heart, however, the Holy Spirit will bring them to your mind when you need them most. This is the case when I minister to women through Dashing Dish. Instead of my having to dig through the Bible to find an encouraging word, oftentimes the Holy Spirit will give me a specific promise that brings refreshment to their souls.

Jesus contradicted the lies and temptation of Satan using God's spoken Word, and the Holy Spirit will remind us of the Word when we are tempted. We are then able to open our mouth and use the two-edged sword to combat the enemy and be victorious (see Heb. 4:12). Every time I am faced with a tempting situation, I have learned to open my mouth and say, "Get behind me, Satan, for it is written…"

The good news is that we not only have the Word of God to overcome temptation, we also have the same Spirit of God that empowered Jesus inside us when we were born again. Romans 8:11 confirms this, saying, "The Spirit of God, who raised Jesus from the dead, lives in you." Just take a moment and think about that! The power that raised Jesus from the dead is inside you and me! That means we have no reason to go around feeling defeated by temptation, but instead can feel empowered knowing that God has given us all we need to be victorious over sin.

Strengthening Our Spiritual Muscles

Learning to yield to the Spirit doesn't necessarily happen overnight, and it certainly requires some training. However, much like bearing fruit, this isn't something we have to accomplish in our own strength. The Holy Spirit was given to us as our helper Who will guide us every step of the way.

We also have the promise that as we submit ourselves to God and resist the enemy, He must flee from us (see James 4:7). The more we yield ourselves to God's leading and resist the Devil (and his temptations), the stronger we become in the Spirit. As we get stronger, we will be better equipped to recognize and resist temptation as it comes to us. I like to think of these actions (submitting and resisting) as a form of training that strengthens our spiritual muscles.

I will never forget when God gave me a very clear depiction of this type of training. At the time I was doing a kickboxing class a few times a week. These classes were a great cardiovascular workout that incorporated great music, dancing, and boxing. The hour-long class got my blood pumping as I jabbed, kicked, and punched away. One day, in the middle of the class, I looked through the window and noticed some people lifting weights in the weight room. One guy in particular caught my attention, because he was lifting dumbbells that looked to be half the size of my body.

This got me thinking about my fitness goals. Although I was in pretty good cardiovascular shape, I was lacking strength. Before that day I had never set foot in a weight room. I knew I needed to have a balanced exercise routine to obtain optimal health, so I decided to incorporate some weight lifting. At first I felt a bit discouraged because I could barely lift five- to ten-pound dumbbells. As I stayed consistent with my routine, however, my muscles eventually became stronger. My workouts started to get a little easier over time, and before I knew it, I was able to increase the weight I was lifting.

The Lord used this to show me that strengthening my "spiritual muscles" is much like strengthening my physical muscles at the gym. As we consistently resist the flesh and say no to sinful habits and behaviors, it will only be a matter of time before we become strong in the Spirit and those things are easy to deny.

There are some practical ways we can build our "spiritual muscles" to resist temptation that might harm our physical bodies. We can make healthy choices when dining out, pass on unhealthy snacks and desserts at the office and parties, and enjoy treats one or two times a week rather than daily. These simple choices may seem insignificant, but over time the act of saying no strengthens our spiritual muscles.

It might seem uncomfortable to make some of these decisions at first, especially if our flesh is used to getting its way. (Remember that untrained two-year-old?) As you practice moderation, however, you will eventually find that your flesh won't cry out quite as loud as it used to, much like a child who is learning they can't always get their way.

Perseverance

The last and final thing that we will be discussing in this chapter is the foundation we need to grow in any area: perseverance.

I believe that it is part of our human nature to want change quickly and without effort. In fact, one of the traits of our flesh is that we want something, and we want it now!

Yet as difficult as it may seem, we all have the ability to walk in patience, diligence, and self-control. Every time we make the choice to yield to the Spirit of God inside us, we will be able to stand strong in the Lord and gain victory over our flesh and the enemy.

Just as we know that it takes time and perseverance to build muscle and strength, so it is with strengthening our spiritual muscles. With every decision that we make to obey and follow the Spirit's leading, our spiritual strength will increase, making it easier to resist the pull of the flesh. As we continue to allow the Holy Spirit to lead us, our ability to hear from God and follow His lead will become as easy and habitual as breathing.

God Will Always Provide a Way Out

In this life we have a daily choice to yield ourselves either to sin or to God. The moment we were born again, God gave us a new nature that has the power to overcome sin. Although we will always have the flesh to contend with as long as we remain in our physical bodies, we no longer have to be controlled or enslaved by sin. Romans 6:11–13 tells you that you should "consider yourselves to be dead to the power of sin and alive to God through Christ Jesus. Do not let sin control the way you live; do not give in to sinful desires. Do not let any part of your body become an instrument of evil to serve sin. Instead, give yourselves completely to God, for you were dead, but now you have new life. So use your whole body as an instrument to do what is right for the glory of God."

The next time you are facing a temptation, know that freedom can be found as we yield ourselves to the Spirit of God within us. Our Heavenly Father promises that we will never be tempted beyond what we are able to bear, and that with all temptation, He will always provide a means of escape (see 1 Cor. 10:13). When we turn to the Lord in repentance, stay faithful in prayer, and renew our minds, we will have victory over sin and finally be able to say no to that plate of cookies!

FOOD FOR THOUGHT

Nourishment for the Soul

Scripture

Throw off your old sinful nature and your former way of life, which is corrupted by lust and deception. Instead, let the Spirit renew your thoughts and attitudes. Put on your new nature, created to be like God—truly righteous and holy (Eph. 4:22–24).

Reflection Questions

- Can you see yourself acting like that two-year-old throwing a temper tantrum in any area of your life? Do you feel that you struggle with giving in to the flesh as it relates to caring for your body/health?
- What are the benefits to walking by the Spirit of God? What are three ways you can walk by the Spirit rather than gratify the desires of the flesh?

■ What are some practical ways you can build your "spiritual muscles" to resist temptation when it comes to caring for your physical body?

Prayer

Dear Lord, I ask that You would help me renew my mind, stay faithful in prayer, and walk in Your ways. When I start to drift off the path that You have for my life in any area, help me to be quick to repent and submit myself to You. I know that as I follow Your will, a deep sense of peace will be produced in my life. Therefore I submit myself to Your leading. I thank You for the Holy Spirit, Who leads and guides me into all truth and gives me the victory over my old sinful nature. I ask that You would help me to be quick to recognize when I am being tempted with unhealthy thoughts, actions, or behaviors, and that You would strengthen me to follow Your will rather than my flesh. Father, I thank You that You are helping me to put off the behaviors and mind-sets of my flesh, and that You are teaching me to put on my new self, created after the likeness of God in true righteousness and holiness. In Jesus' Name, amen.

Nourishment for the Body
Chicken Caesar Lettuce Wraps

This recipe is fresh, delicious, and perfect for a light lunch or dinner. It has a healthier Caesar dressing, and it comes together quickly since your slow cooker does all the work. The lettuce wraps can also be swapped out for a whole grain bun or wrap bread.

Ingredients

1½ pounds fresh or frozen
    chicken breast

1 cup chicken stock (or 1
    chicken bouillon cube
    and 1 cup water)

Caesar Dressing:

1 cup plain low-fat Greek
    yogurt
½ cup Parmesan cheese,
    grated
1 tablespoon Worcestershire
    sauce
1 teaspoon garlic powder
½ teaspoon onion powder

½ teaspoon mustard
1½ tablespoons lemon juice
    (or juice of 1 lemon)
1 tablespoon white wine
    vinegar
½ teaspoon salt
½ teaspoon pepper

Lettuce Wraps:

8 romaine lettuce leaves, rinsed and dried

Method

To prepare chicken: Place the chicken breasts in a slow cooker with chicken broth (or bouillon cube and water). Cover and place on high heat for about 3 hours, or low heat for 6 hours (4 hours on high heat or 8 hours on low heat for frozen chicken), or until chicken is cooked through and is tender enough that it can be easily shredded. Remove the chicken from the slow cooker and pull apart with two forks until it is shredded to your liking. (If you're using precooked chicken you can skip this step. You can also do this well in advance and keep the shredded chicken in your fridge for up to 7 days.) To prepare Caesar dressing: Place all the ingredients for the dressing in a small bowl and whisk together or puree in a blender until smooth and creamy.

Toss the shredded chicken in the Caesar dressing and place on romaine lettuce leaves, dividing chicken mixture into 8 servings (about ¼ heaping cup per lettuce wrap). Or divide the chicken mixture among 4 whole grain tortillas or buns, if desired (about ½ heaping cup chicken mixture over each sandwich). Top with additional Parmesan cheese and black pepper, if desired.

Yields: 4 servings

7

NOURISHING THE BODY

When it comes to food, it's not all about saying no. In fact, I believe God created food to be both nourishing and enjoyable! If we take a look around our grocery's produce section, for example, we can clearly see that God created food to be satisfying to our senses. Have you ever stopped and noticed all the colors, smells, tastes, and visually beautiful food He created for us to nourish our body with?

Despite the fact that God created food to be good, I believe that many of us have a distorted view of food. This could be a result of diets, disordered eating, issues with our weight, or something in our past. Much as we did with the health of our soul, let's take a moment to dig up any misconceived thought patterns we have about food and lay a new foundation for nourishing our body based on God's design.

One of the best ways to abolish misconceptions is by replacing them with practical facts. Unfortunately, the overabundance of information available today about food and nutrition often leaves us feeling uncertain about what actions to take. In order to optimize the way we view food and our body, we first need to counter many of the misunderstandings we have accumulated over the years.

Ditch the Diets

Many of the skewed perceptions that we have about food come from the diet industry. As I mentioned in previous chapters, the problem with diets is that they are always changing, making it nearly impossible to distinguish fact from theory.

In addition, diets are often impossible to maintain over the long term, which is a guaranteed recipe for failure. If you have ever taken a ride on the diet roller coaster, you may already know that the results produced from a diet are just that: a high (hooray, I've lost weight) followed by an inevitable low (oh no, I've gained the weight back and then some).

This recurring failure is the reason the diet industry makes billions of dollars each year. The worst part of all is that the money invested in these "quick fixes" often comes from well-meaning people who want to improve their health. Because so many people are overwhelmed and confused about how to do so, they often buy into false promises. If you are one of the people who have tried countless diets and failed, take heart, because there is a better way!

Now, before I go any further, I want to start by saying that I am not against having a plan. In fact, I believe that planning and setting goals are beneficial and necessary when we set out to make a change. I also want to clarify that I am not against diets that people must go on because of food intolerances, allergies, etc., and I am certainly not against programs or tools that help people live a healthy lifestyle long term.

What I am in disagreement with, however, are the diets that promote an unhealthy and unbalanced approach to losing weight. Why am I personally so against diets? There are countless reasons, but one of the main ones is that I have seen the vicious cycle of defeat that they have produced in countless women. I also can also speak from personal experience when it comes to dieting, because, as I mentioned, I bought into many of the unhealthy diet trends when I was battling eating disorders.

I'll never forget when someone innocently shared the false (and incomplete) theory with me that bread makes a person gain weight. In my desperate attempt to control my weight, I decided that if cutting out bread would make me skinnier, then I would cut out all carbohydrates. This example demonstrates how a theory (which may have some truth to it) can be taken to an unhealthy extreme in an effort to produce quick results.

I believe that this is how many diet trends begin. There may be some truth in them, but they are often taken to an extreme in order to produce instant gratification. The reality of all unbalanced theories, however, is that they are all bound to produce failure and defeat in the long run.

Laying a New Foundation

After years of disordered eating I decided that there must be a better way. It wasn't until I laid down all the thoughts and theories I had about food that I was able to find God's perfect plan for my body. At the time it was difficult to let go of any preconceived notions, but I can now see that it was one of the best decisions I've made about my health. I encourage you to do the same. Once we make the choice to clear out any previous way of thinking, we can lay new groundwork for promoting our health and maintaining a healthy balance.

Most of us know that in order to achieve our health and fitness goals, we need to eat a variety of nutritious foods. However, because of the many nutritional labels on food, most of us are unclear about which foods are actually healthy. It can also be difficult to determine the right balance of nutrients to consume in order to optimize our individual metabolism and health.

The Basics of Clean Eating

Instead of making things more complicated by providing more facts, statistics, and information (which can only further the confusion), I want to present a simple and logical way to decide what foods are best for our health. I believe we can easily determine the best food to eat by thinking about what God intended for us to eat from the very beginning. This essentially means choosing food that is in its most natural state.

This is generally referred to as "clean eating," which essentially means eating food that hasn't been processed or altered in any way. There are many benefits to clean eating, some of the most common being weight loss, increased energy, and improved digestion. *Please keep in mind that just as with any term pertaining to a style of eating, everyone has a slightly different opinion of what foods are "clean." The opinions expressed in this book are based on general health standards, and may need to be modified to fit your specific needs.*

In general, clean eating is a simple way of identifying real foods that nourish the physical body. This way of eating is not a diet, but rather a lifestyle approach that incorporates whole foods that haven't been processed or altered with chemicals.

An easy way to determine if something is processed is to check the ingredients list. If something has white flour, added sugar, unhealthy sources of fat, or is filled with chemicals or preservatives (generally in the form of words you can't pronounce), it probably isn't the best for your health.

The Nutritional Breakdown of Food

In order to determine how to properly fuel our bodies, let's start by looking at the basic nutritional components of food: macronutrients.

Calories: It is important to start by clearing up any misconceptions that we may have had about food, starting with calories. Calories are not the enemy, despite what you may have believed in the past. Simply put, the amount of calories in a serving of food tells us how much energy that food will provide for our body's use. Paying attention to calories allows us to make wise decisions about how to fuel our body daily. I like to think of calories as an energy budget that we need for our day. Once we determine the amount of calories we need, we will be able to determine how to best fuel our individual body. Getting too few or too many calories in a day (especially when it happens often) can harm our bodies, weight, and overall health.

Carbohydrates: Just like calories, carbohydrates can get a bad rap, but they are certainly not the enemy. In fact, carbohydrates are vital for fueling our brain, muscles, and body. When it comes to carbohydrates, it is important to focus on both the source and the amount to meet your specific goals and needs. In general, the Dietary Guidelines for Americans recommends that carbohydrates make up 45 to 65 percent of your total daily calories. This equates to between two hundred and three hundred grams of carbohydrates a day, depending on how many calories you need per day. To determine the amount of carbohydrates you need, it is important to think about multiple factors such as your age, height, body weight, gender, as well as your activity level and lifestyle. If you have a very active occupation such as a waitress for example, you may need more carbohydrates for fuel than someone who sits at a desk all day. Once you get a general idea of how many carbohydrates you need, you can check the nutrition label and determine if the amount of carbohydrates is right for your body's needs.

As far as the source of carbohydrates, there are two to pick from: complex and simple. Complex carbohydrates are certainly the better of the two because they are slow to digest due to their high fiber content, making them a more sustainable source of energy, as well as one that has less of an impact on your blood glucose levels. The best type of complex carbohydrates to look for is whole grains, which include oats, beans, and lentils. Fruits and vegetables, like apples and broccoli, also offer great complex carbs. Simple carbohydrates, on the other hand, are typically high in sugar, white flour, and processed ingredients (think cupcakes, pastries, and candy). They are digested very quickly, which provides a quick energy boost followed by a crash. If you have ever been the victim of a midday energy slump, simple carbohydrates are most likely the culprit. It is best to limit them, or cut them out altogether.

Fiber: The next thing you will want to look for is the amount of fiber in a serving. Complex carbohydrate foods are typically higher in fiber than simple carbohydrates. This is especially helpful to keep in mind when you are choosing a bread or pasta product, for example. I try to look for the one with a lot of fiber because it will digest at a slower rate, providing my body with a sustained source of energy. Some good sources of fiber are the complex carbohydrates listed above.

Protein: Protein is essential for the building of lean muscle tissue, and it is also the macronutrient that takes the longest to digest. This means it keeps us feeling satisfied for a longer duration of time. When I look at the amount of protein in a food, I check to see if it has at least as much protein in a serving as it does carbohydrates. If it does, I know it is a well-balanced food and a good source of protein. Some good sources of protein are lean meats, fish, low-fat dairy products, and eggs.

Fats: As with carbohydrates, there are many misconceptions about fats. Contrary to popular belief, not all fat will make you fat. There are different types, some beneficial to your health, others harmful in large amounts. The good kinds of fats, such as the omegas and mono/polyunsaturated fats, are important for your brain and nervous function as well as cardiovascular health. Healthy fats are also digested more slowly, which can help keep you feeling satisfied. Foods with healthy fats include salmon, avocado, nuts, nut butters, and olive oil. Saturated fats, on the other hand, can have harmful effects on our cardiovascular system. Therefore they should be limited in your diet, if not cut out altogether. Some examples are high-fat cuts of beef, lamb, pork, chicken with skin, whole milk, cream, butter, cheese, and ice cream. Additionally, many baked goods and fried foods are high in saturated fat.

Sugar: When it comes to refined sugars, I recommend keeping your consumption as low as possible. Refined sugar does not benefit your body nutritionally in any way. I personally have found that the more sugar I consume, the more sugar I crave. Sugar can also negatively affect your blood glucose levels, energy levels, and more. I recommend looking for foods that are sweetened with natural sweeteners, including stevia, honey, pure maple syrup, agave nectar, and raw cane sugar, because they will affect your body in a different way from white or processed sugars.

As you can see, there is a lot to take into account when it comes to the nutritional breakdown of foods. But don't let it overwhelm you. The main thing you want to pay attention to is getting a good balance of complex carbohydrates, healthy fats, and lean proteins throughout your day. In addition, limit (or eliminate) the simple carbohydrates, refined sugar, and unhealthy fats from your diet.

Keeping a Food Diary

If you want your body to function optimally, it is good to pay attention to overall calories, but it is equally important to pay attention to where the calories are coming from. An easy way of tracking whether you are consuming the right amount of calories for your body and ensuring you are getting a good balance of nutrients is keeping a food diary, whether using a pen and notebook or an online food tracker. Of course, I present this recommendation with caution, since I know that food tracking can cause obsessive tendencies if taken to the extreme.

To ensure that food journaling doesn't become an unhealthy behavior, I recommend tracking your food for about two to four weeks. This is typically just enough time to become familiar with the foods you are consuming regularly. It will also help you identify any unhealthy eating behaviors, such as mindless or emotional eating, as well as identify the triggers. Food journaling can also be a great way to become familiar with the calories, macronutrients, and serving sizes of the foods you consume regularly.

Keeping a food diary will also help you determine if you are getting a good balance of the macronutrients in your diet. For example, if your entire day's food record shows that you ate only one serving of protein, you know that you need to focus on getting more lean protein throughout your day. You may also notice that you are eating more processed foods than whole foods. You can then make changes to your meals to make them more nutritionally dense and balanced.

As you make the changes necessary to nourish your body, it will respond in a positive way almost immediately. When your body is fueled properly, its natural hunger signals and energy levels operate just as God designed them. These God-given tools provide you with the signals to stay on track and consume the proper amount of calories each day. (This also eliminates the need for a food journal, which is why I suggest keeping one for only a short period at the beginning of your journey to health.) Following the design that God intended for your body frees you from the need to diet, count calories, and become obsessive or overwhelmed about food choices and your body.

My Journey to Clean Eating

I started to experience the benefits of clean eating on a personal level while I was in nursing school. At that point in my journey, I was tired of dieting, and my God-given love for cooking had just started to develop. I also became fascinated with the human body, and wanted to learn more about the role food plays in our health.

I remember going to the campus library after class almost every day and reading everything I could find about nutrition. As I started doing research, I quickly noticed a common theme among almost everything I read: white flour and sugar can negatively impact our energy levels, weight, and overall health. I also discovered that supposedly healthier substitutions for white flour, such as whole wheat flour, are still processed, and are not much better.

I decided to take what I had learned and apply it to my own life, testing if what I had read would really make a difference. I started by cutting out processed sugar and white and whole wheat flour, and replacing them with natural sweeteners and whole grains.

I started making my own oat flour to replace the white and whole wheat. Oat flour can be made at home using old-fashioned oats by blending them in a food processor or blender. I also found a naturally sweet herb called stevia, which replaced the sugar in my kitchen. Within a few weeks of making these changes, I noticed that I was less bloated, I had more stable energy levels, and all my clothes got looser without an intentional effort to lose weight.

I carried this newfound knowledge over to the kitchen, where I began to construct recipes without any white flour or sugar. I got rid of all of the processed foods in my pantry and refrigerator, and swapped them out for whole foods that are naturally made. With just a few simple swaps, I quickly found that all the foods I enjoyed could be made in a much healthier way without losing any of their flavor.

This discovery opened a whole new world for me. I no longer felt I had to restrict foods like ice cream, pizza, or pasta. Instead I learned to make all my favorite foods using ingredients that satisfied my taste buds and allowed my body to feel its best. The best part of all was that I finally started to view food as something both enjoyable and nourishing to my body, just as God intended.

Some of the swaps I made in my kitchen are:

- Oat flour or almond flour instead of white or wheat flour
- Stevia or honey instead of sugar
- Spaghetti squash, zucchini noodles, or quinoa- or lentil-based pasta instead of white or whole wheat pasta
- Greek yogurt or applesauce instead of butter or oil
- Low-sugar snacks made with a balance of whole grains, healthy fats, and protein, such as low-fat Greek yogurt with berries, fruit with nut butter or string cheese, or vegetables and hummus rather than processed crackers or chips

To this day I am still finding new ways to swap out unhealthy ingredients for wholesome foods, and having a lot of fun creating recipes as I discover them! You can find some great ideas on my blog, www.dashingdish.com. I recommend to anyone looking to get started with making healthy swaps to start by removing all "white" foods from your pantry and fridge. This includes foods with sugar and white flour such as processed crackers and chips, sugary cereals, white bread, pasta, and processed baked goods. Not only do these foods lack nutritional benefits, they also tend to be the foods that are the most addicting and lead to more cravings.

Change Your Focus with Food

This doesn't mean that you need to eat perfectly "clean" all the time, or that you need to swear off all sugar and processed foods. Rather, it is about finding balance and moderation that you can live with over the long term. For me this meant making the choice to cook and prepare healthy wholesome meals the majority of the time, while still going out to eat maybe once a week or having a treat on occasion.

That being said, as much as I enjoy special treats from time to time, I have found that I actually enjoy the healthy dishes I make at home. And while an occasional ice cream cone tastes wonderful while I'm eating it, it typically doesn't take long for me to feel lousy afterward. Not only does it leave me feeling bloated and sleepy, it also leaves me craving more. Isn't it strange how sugar makes us want a second or even third helping, and yet we never seem to feel that way after eating broccoli?

As I started to notice how much better wholesome foods made my body feel, many of the processed foods started to lose their appeal. This was quite a shift from the way I used to think, when I was focusing on the foods I *couldn't* have. I soon realized I would rather feel satisfied and nourished after a meal than indulge my flesh and regret it afterward.

Clean Eating Is a Way of Life

When I started this journey to eat clean, I decided to stop dieting once and for all. Instead I aimed to eat three meals per day with a balance of complex carbohydrates, lean protein, and a small portion of healthy fat. I also enjoyed one or two protein-rich snacks that satisfied my hunger in between meals.

This was a dramatic difference from the way I used to eat. I remember starving my body for as long as I could between meals, believing I was controlling my weight by ignoring my hunger. Now I never let myself get overly hungry, knowing that it causes me to lose any sense of my body's natural hunger signals and often leads to overeating. I have learned to keep my body fueled with something nutritious every few hours, which not only keeps my blood sugar stable but also keeps my cravings at bay.

As you can see, clean eating is not a diet, nor is it a short-term plan or program. Rather, clean eating means nourishing your body with food that God created. As you make clean eating your new way of life, you will learn to appreciate the natural flavor of foods as they were meant to be consumed.

The best part of living a healthy lifestyle (rather than going on a diet) is that it allows flexibility, balance, and moderation, making it maintainable over the long term.

As you make the necessary changes to nourish your body, you will begin to notice how your body starts to work just as God designed it. You may even start to notice improvements in your energy level and overall health in just a few short weeks. Over time you will begin to develop healthy habits that will soon become a new way of life. It won't take long before you find yourself enjoying food in a balanced way, and you'll radiate health from the inside out!

FOOD FOR THOUGHT

Nourishment for the Soul

Scripture

All the animals of the earth, all the birds of the sky, all the small animals that scurry along the ground, and all the fish in the sea will look on you with fear and terror. I have placed them in your power. I have given them to you for food, just as I have given you grain and vegetables (Gen. 9:2–3).

Reflection Questions

- Do you believe that God intended food to be enjoyed? Why or why not?
- Have you ever been on a diet or followed a popular trend as it relates to food? What was the outcome?

- How can clean eating help you find God's design as it relates to caring for your body?
- After learning about the benefits of clean eating, what are some of the steps that you plan to take to improve your nutrition and start living a healthier lifestyle?

Prayer

Dear Lord, I thank You for making foods of all different shapes, textures, smells, and tastes for our enjoyment. Please give me a desire for the whole, fresh foods that You created to nourish my body, and help me to be willing to let go of anything that is not beneficial to my health. Please show me if there is anything I need to change in my diet that is not beneficial for my health, or if I have any lingering mind-sets about food that are not pleasing to You. Father, please help me to clear out all the misconceptions and confusion that I may have about food, and replace them with Your perfect plan. As I seek to make changes, I ask You for wisdom. I ask that You bless all my efforts, and that You guide me every step of the way in my journey to health. In Jesus' Name, amen.

Nourishment for the Body
Chocolate Chip Banana Bread Snack Cake

This cake is absolutely one of my favorite snacks, but it also makes a great on-the-go breakfast or dessert. This clean-eating snack cake tastes like a piece of banana bread, without the flour, sugar, or butter!

Ingredients

Nonstick cooking spray
3 medium ripe bananas,
    mashed (about 1 cup)
1 cup unsweetened
    applesauce
1 large egg
½ cup baking stevia (or 1 cup
    sweetener that measures
    like sugar)

1¾ cups oat flour
1 teaspoon baking powder
½ teaspoon baking soda
½ teaspoon salt
¼ cup dark chocolate chips
    (I like to use stevia-
    sweetened chocolate
    chips)

Method

Preheat oven to 350 degrees. Spray a 9-by-9-inch baking dish with cooking spray.

Add all the ingredients to a medium bowl and stir to combine.

Pour mixture into baking pan and bake for 20 to 25 minutes, or until a toothpick comes out clean. Let cool and cut into 9 squares. Store in the fridge until ready to serve.

Yields: 9 servings

8
PUTTING IT ALL INTO PRACTICE

hen it comes to living a healthy lifestyle, we have learned that we need to take both a spiritual and a physical approach to wellness. I believe that when we address both components together, we will discover the fullness of the healthy life we so greatly desire.

Yet, even with all the knowledge in the world, it may seem nearly impossible to live out what we know we should do. In moments like these we often want to know, how do I put everything I have learned into practice?

When I started my journey to health, I too felt over-whelmed. After spending months studying how to best care for my body and soul, I had a lot of information, but I also needed to know how to apply it in a practical way. One of the things that helped me immensely was writing down my short-term goals. Doing so allowed me to see my overall goal broken down into smaller realistic steps.

To help myself reach my health-related goals (without feeling burdened), I decided to make a list of ways I could practically nourish my body and soul. Here are ten keys to living a healthy lifestyle that are just as easy to remember as they are to put into practice!

1. Partner with God and Others

When we set out to accomplish a goal, we often make one of two errors. We either try to do everything on our own, relying on our own wisdom, strength, and ability, or we pray and ask God to help us but fail to do our part. I have found that it is only when we actively engage in a partnership with God that the impossible suddenly becomes possible. After all, He never intended us to do anything on our own, so it would be foolish to imagine that we can accomplish anything apart from Him.

One of my favorite depictions of our partnership with God is found in Matthew 14:13–21. In this passage Jesus sends the disciples on a mission to feed thousands of men, women, and children. At the time the disciples don't see any way of doing so, because they're contemplating feeding the multitude in their own strength and ability. Jesus sees their lack of faith and tells them, "That isn't necessary. *You* feed them."

The disciples explain that they have only five loaves of bread and two fish, which aren't nearly enough to feed everyone. Jesus responds by telling them to bring what they have to Him. He then blesses the bread and fish and hands them back to the disciples to distribute to the people. They all eat as much as they want, and there is even some left over!

This is a beautiful display of how Jesus can take what we have and multiply our efforts, ability, and provisions. We can see that although Jesus could have fed the multitudes single-handedly, He involved the disciples, giving them a crucial role. It was only when the disciples gave Jesus what they had in their hands that He was willing to bless and multiply it.

Likewise, the disciples had an active role in distributing the food to the people.

This is such a powerful display of the partnership we have with the Lord. Just as with all partnerships, there is a part for each of us to play. We do our part by inviting God to walk with us in our journey. By giving Him what we have in our hands, we trust Him to help us in our areas of weakness.

You can invite God into your situation through prayer, spending time with Him, listening to and obeying Him, and continually seeking His wisdom every step of the way. I believe seeking God for guidance pleases Him greatly. He always responds by sending help from the Holy Spirit, Who is our guide, counselor, and friend.

This specifically applies to living a healthy lifestyle, because it requires not only wisdom from God but also our obedience and cooperation. For example, we are the ones who must make the choice to buy nutritious groceries, lace up our tennis shoes to go for a run, and order healthy food when dining out. As we ask for wisdom on how to care for our body, and act on what He is leading us to do, He is able to bless and multiply our efforts.

In addition to partnering with God, it can be incredibly valuable to partner with others in our journey to health. Just as we were never meant to do anything apart from God, I also believe He never intended us to be isolated and achieve every goal on our own.

Having a support system in place is especially helpful on the days when we are lacking motivation or are tempted to quit. I personally found this to be true when my sister and I started working out together. There were days when I didn't feel like going to the gym, but knowing that my sister was meeting me gave me the accountability I needed to stay committed.

When we join with others, we are able to share our struggles, gain practical advice, and encourage one another. Whether we find support from a family member, friend, or support group, there is strength in numbers!

2. Pray over Your Food

Many of us grew up eating our meals around the dinner table, but in our busy society, a sit-down meal is quickly becoming a thing of the past. These days people are eating on the go, eating while standing up, and eating in the car more than ever. Oftentimes this means we forget to take the time to relax, enjoy, and pray over our food.

If this sounds familiar, I would encourage you to take the time to sit down and pray before you eat. Personally, I like to thank God for my food and ask Him to bless it to my body's use. I also pray and ask Him to help me listen to the hunger cues He has placed within me. When we pray over our food, we are essentially inviting the Lord to the table with us. This changes our mealtimes from something solely about us to something He can bless.

I have found that when we invite God in with the small things, we suddenly become aware of His presence in every area of our lives. It is then that He is able to lead and guide us to make the best choices for our health and overall well-being.

3. Pitch the Junk

One of my first recommendations for living a healthy lifestyle is to start by cleaning out the fridge and pantry and pitching the junk food! As we discussed in previous chapters, junk food is anything processed and lacking nutritional benefit to our bodies. Man-made processed foods are not only void of nutrition, they are often filled with sugar, sodium, and additives, which leave us craving more. Replacing these foods with fruits, vegetables, whole grains, lean protein, and healthy fats will not only keep cravings at bay, but also benefit the whole body.

As you clean out your kitchen, I also recommend cleaning out anything that is tempting to you personally. I am not suggesting that you never eat your favorite foods again, but I do think it is best to keep them out of your house. This eliminates any unnecessary temptations and makes it more enjoyable when you do have them on occasion.

For me personally, temptation equates to peanut butter ice cream, but because I don't keep it in my house, I don't have to resist it! Instead I fill my freezer with healthier treats like frozen strawberries that I mash into plain Greek yogurt, and it tastes almost as good as ice cream! Then, on occasion, my husband and I will go out for ice cream and I will help myself to peanut butter!

Whether you are like me and enjoy ice cream, or you are a pizza or nachos kind of gal, I recommend that you become familiar with the things that are a weakness to your flesh. Do yourself a huge favor and keep them out of your house, reserving them for special occasions.

Now, that being said, I don't suggest that you banish your favorite foods from your kitchen altogether. Instead I recommend making healthier versions of the things that you enjoy throughout the week. If you desire pizza, for example, make a homemade oat flour pizza crust (a recipe can be found in the "Food for Thought" section at the end of this chapter), and top it with tomato sauce, a little cheese, and lots of vegetables. I strongly believe that finding healthier alternatives to the foods you enjoy is essential for maintaining a healthy lifestyle over the long term, which is why I have a passion for creating delicious clean-eating recipes on Dashing Dish!

4. Process Your Emotions

There was a time when I would run to food for comfort when we are emotional, bored, tired, or stressed. Since I have begun to be more mindful of what and why I am eating, I have changed the way I respond to my emotions when it comes to food. It didn't happen overnight, but as I learned to walk by the Spirit (as we discussed in chapter 6), I found victory over emotional and mindless eating.

One of the steps I took to change my emotional response to food was taking a moment to process how I am feeling. By taking that moment, I am able to ask myself: Am I eating for comfort? Am I turning to food to bring myself temporary satisfaction, or to procrastinate from something? Or am I really hungry? Taking a moment to ask yourself these honest questions will give you the time you need to make a course correction.

When you realize that you are turning to food out of emotion, it gives you the opportunity to physically stop, turn around, and head out of the kitchen. This will allow you to remove yourself from the tempting situation and find somewhere to spend time with Jesus, even if it means getting in your car, taking a walk, or going into your bedroom.

I also like to take a few moments to process how I feel while I am eating. I do this by asking myself, Am I eating mindlessly or am I truly hungry? Am I satisfied yet? If the answer is yes, I am able to put down my fork and remove myself from the situation until I am able to deal with my emotions in a healthy way.

When we make the choice to run to God instead of food, He will meet our needs and satisfy our souls in a way that only He can. And we won't have the regrets that come with emotional eating, which are so often piled on top of whatever we were trying to bury in the first place. God wants us to run to Him for comfort, and He promises that when we do, He will comfort us and give us a renewed sense of joy and hope (see Ps. 94:19).

5. Plan

When it comes to living a healthy lifestyle, I am convinced that planning is key! Planning prevents us from making bad choices when we are hungry, stressed, or pressed for time. One of my favorite ways to do it is to meal plan. Meal planning can be as simple or as complex as you want to make it. You can start small by packing your lunches, or by preparing your meats and washing your produce to quickly add to recipes throughout the week. You can also plan on a broader scale by preparing multiple meals for the week ahead.

When it comes to meal planning, I fall somewhere in between these two options. Typically, I take a few hours on a Sunday or Monday to prepare my meats, wash and cut my vegetables, and boil some quinoa pasta to throw into recipes throughout the week. I also like to bake up a batch of clean-eating muffins and a few other snacks to have on hand when I am busy or on the go.

Another important part of planning is getting organized by preparing a grocery list and meal plan. I like to use my Dashing Dish Meal Plan Builder and Grocery List Builder to plan what I will be having for the week. As I plug my recipes into the meal plan builder, the ingredients go straight to my grocery list, which then syncs with the Dashing Dish iPhone app. I love having my calendar and grocery list with me on my phone at the grocery store, as well as having the ability to print them off at home to hang on my fridge. This keeps me organized and on track, and it saves me time, stress, and money throughout the week.

Last but not least, I strongly suggest planning ahead when you know you're going to have a busy day. When hunger strikes and you aren't prepared, it often leads to trips through the drive-through, or overeating when you arrive at home because you are overly hungry. A better option is to have a plan and pack a meal or high-protein snack to take with you. Some of my favorite packable snacks are apples, almonds, cheese sticks, and homemade clean-eating baked goods. Having healthy snacks on hand can prevent you from making unwise choices in the moment or overeating later.

6. Portion Control

In our supersize society, portion control can be tricky. This is why I suggest food journaling for a few weeks in order to learn what a cup, ounce, and gram actually look like. (You may even want to buy a food scale in order to really educate yourself.) Once you have a relative idea of what a serving size looks like, the challenge is sticking to those portions.

One of the ways I have found it helpful to eat smaller portions, yet feel satisfied, is by bulking up my meal with low-calorie fruits and vegetables. Sure, four ounces of cooked chicken may not seem like a lot of food, but when placed on a big bowl of greens along with a bunch of other toppings such as fresh vegetables, it seems much more satisfying to both your eyes and stomach.

Another way to stay satisfied and maintain portion control is by staying properly hydrated. Often we mistake thirst for hunger, so filling up on water and water-rich foods, such as fruits and vegetables, can help keep us feeling full. The important thing about choosing beverages is that you stick to ones that don't add calories or sugar to your diet. Tea, decaf coffee, sparkling water, and lemon water are all great options. I have also found that it is much easier to mind portion sizes when I am eating a few small snacks throughout the day. When I have a snack that is rich in protein, fiber, and healthy fats, I find that I am better able to pay attention to my body's hunger cues when I sit down to eat a meal.

Special occasions and holidays are another area where portion sizes can be challenging. Special occasions are typically filled with a lot of food and special treats, some of which come around only once a year. In these moments I suggest picking one of your favorite treats, such as one of your grandma's homemade cookies, or one piece of your mom's famous pie. The problem comes when people feel that they need to savor every bit of food put in front of them. I also recommend practicing portion control by filling up with healthier options (either before or during the party), then carefully choosing a single serving of one treat that you really want to enjoy.

Last but not least, when it comes to portion control, it is important to be mindful at restaurants. The good news is, these days there are a lot more options when it comes to ordering smaller portion sizes, as well as healthier options on the menu. What do you do, however, when a lighter option is not available? One way to mind your portion size while eating out is to eat slowly and pay attention to when you are truly satisfied (not stuffed), and take the rest home with you. You can also split an entree or dessert with someone.

7. Priorities

I think that it's pretty safe to say that we women tend to neglect ourselves in an effort to care for those around us. Somehow we tend to think that making our health a priority is selfish. Yet, this could not be further from the truth!

I am often reminded of what flight attendants say about caring for ourselves first in the event of an emergency. Before takeoff they explain that if you are traveling with small children, you need to put your own oxygen mask on before putting one on anyone else. They often remind us that although it may seem illogical, if we don't take care of ourselves, we won't be there to care for those who need us.

It's time we realize that in order to be the best wife, mom, caretaker, businesswoman, etc. we can be, we need to prioritize our health so we can be healthy enough to care for others. It's time we gave ourselves permission to care for our body, knowing that it is worth taking care of.

One of my favorite ways to make my health a priority is by dedicating the first hour of my day to spending time with the Lord, followed by a quick and effective workout (more on this in chapter 10). When I start my day with the Lord and moving my body, everything I do later in the day is more productive. I find that I have more energy and strength to get through my day, and I have the peace of God guarding my heart and mind.

If you think you don't have time to dedicate one or two hours in your day to strengthening yourself spiritually and physically, then I would encourage you to refocus your priorities. Each of us has the same twenty-four hours in a day, and we all get to choose how we are going to spend them. If you want to live a life that is healthy and free, you must make your wellness a priority. Remember, you are worth taking care of and investing in!

8. Perspective

One of the most common temptations for women when it comes to living a healthy lifestyle (as well as in many other areas) is comparison! Thanks to social media, television, and magazines, we are bombarded by multiple sources of comparison every day. When people share pictures of their perfectly clean house, best-dressed kids, and perfectly healthy meals on the Internet, suddenly we feel as if we can never measure up.

There is something so sneaky and subtle about comparing ourselves with others, because so often we can mistake it for inspiration. The only problem is that we often take it a step further and try to be like someone else, which can leave us feeling like a failure.

The problem with comparison as it relates specifically to health and fitness is that every person's body is unique. Various factors dictate a person's body shape and size, such as lifestyle, genetics, hormones, and food sensitivities. The point is, every person's body is different! When we compare ourselves with others in the area of health and fitness, we often make judgments based on external appearance. This is not always an accurate gauge, because someone who is very thin may be unhealthy, and someone who eats healthy and cares for her body may never be a size two! This is just one of the many reasons you can't judge a person's health by her looks, because "healthy" really does look different on everyone.

The most important thing I have learned when it comes to living a healthy lifestyle is to find what works best for me. Being healthy is not about looking like someone else, or following a popular trend. It is about finding and doing what works best to nourish *your* body and care for its specific needs.

Which brings us to the main point: keep it all in perspective! If we spend all our time comparing ourselves with others, we will never be able to run our own race effectively. Instead we will be off on the sidelines wasting time with distractions, and never making progress on our journey.

The next time you are tempted to compare yourself with someone else, choose to re-direct your focus, and instead think about the progress you are making each day. Celebrate each victory, big and small, and keep your eyes focused on the race before you, running with purpose in every step!

9. Purpose

When it comes to living a healthy lifestyle, we all have times in our journey when things get tough. It may be a life change, a stressful season, or a lack of motivation. In times like these, it is important to have a "why" to keep us anchored. Our why is the driving force behind our choice to live a healthy lifestyle, and it is the very reason we started.

If someone were to ask you *why* you desire to live a healthy lifestyle, do you have an answer? Also, is your why sustainable? It is so important to have a viable why for the choices you make, because it is ultimately what will drive and define your actions.

Everyone's why may look different, so it is important to find yours. Perhaps your why is to live a long and healthy life. Maybe your why is to get in shape so you can keep up with your children and family. Or maybe your why is to become the best version of yourself! Whatever it may be, finding the reason you are taking care of yourself will give you a sense of purpose and commitment to keep you going. If you don't yet have a why for making your health a priority, I encourage you to take some time to develop one and write it down.

10. Perseverance

In our society today, we tend to look for quick fixes for everything. If we don't see results overnight, we can quickly become discouraged and impatient. When it comes to learning healthy habits, we have to realize that it often took months, if not years, to develop our current habits, so it will take time to make new ones as well!

One of the keys to overcoming impatience is to develop realistic short-term goals. Start to see every choice (big or small) as a step toward your main goal, and realize that they all add up over time. As you see these short-term goals accomplished, it will bring a sense of empowerment, showing that you are making progress in your journey. This is often what gives us contentment and instills patience along the way.

God also encourages us to be patient, reminding us that when we are diligent and faithful, we will reap a great reward. Galatians 6:9 says, "So let's not get tired of doing what is good. At just the right time we will reap a harvest of blessing if we don't give up." I like to think of every good choice as an act of obedience unto God, knowing that He is cheering me on every step of the way.

Small Steps Bring a Great Reward

These ten keys are not all you need to live a healthy lifestyle, but they are certainly a great foundation to get you started and keep you going strong on your journey! It may not seem like a big deal when you make one of these choices in your daily life, but I have learned that every small step you take adds up to produce lasting change.

Hebrews 10:35–36 encourages us in this same way: "So do not throw away this confident trust in the Lord. Remember the great reward it brings you! Patient endurance is what you need now, so that you will continue to do God's will. Then you will receive all that he has promised." What a great reminder this is to remain steadfast in pursuing God's will, knowing that as we do we will receive all He has promised! When we make the choice to combine daily actions in the physical (taking practical steps toward health) with the spiritual (prayer, reading the Word, and trusting in the Lord), we can be confident that we will receive a great reward!

FOOD FOR THOUGHT

Nourishment for the Soul

Scripture

Don't just listen to God's word. You must do what it says. Otherwise, you are only fooling yourselves (James 1:22).

Reflection Questions

- Do you ever feel that you have an abundance of knowledge when it comes to living a healthy lifestyle, but have a hard time putting it into practice?
- Which of these ten tips do you feel is most helpful in your journey to health? How do you plan on applying them?

Prayer

Dear Lord, thank You for providing me with all the wisdom and guidance I need to get healthy and enjoy the journey! Please help these tips come to my mind when I am tempted to be discouraged, when I get overwhelmed, and when I want to give up. Instead help me to use what I have learned and apply it to my life. I thank You that as I do my part, You will bless all my efforts. In Jesus' Name, amen.

Nourishment for the Body
Homemade Oat Flour Pizza Crust

This whole grain and gluten-free pizza crust will be one of your new favorite ways to enjoy pizza!

Ingredients

Nonstick cooking spray

Dry

1½ cups oat flour (firmly packed)
¼ cup grated Parmesan cheese
¼ teaspoon salt

¼ teaspoon garlic powder
¼ teaspoon Italian seasoning
1½ teaspoons baking powder

Wet

2 large eggs
2 tablespoons honey

2 tablespoons plain low-fat Greek yogurt
1 tablespoon water

Method

Preheat oven to 400°F. Spray a 9-by-9-inch pie dish, round cake pan, or springform pan with cooking spray.

In a medium bowl, combine the dry ingredients first, then add the wet ingredients and stir until dough forms. Press dough into prepared pan.

Bake dough for 10 minutes at 400°F. Take dough out of oven and top with tomato sauce, cheese, veggies, or whatever you desire to put on your pizza. Bake for an additional 5 to 10 minutes, or until cheese is melted to your liking. Remove from oven and cut into 8 slices.

Yields: 8 servings

9

CHANGING YOUR FOCUS OF FOOD

J've had to make many changes over the past several years in regard to my health. As I have made these changes, my relationship with food has also changed. I now view food as fuel, and I have come to find that when I fuel my body correctly, it works the way God intended.

After a few months of making changes to my diet, I noticed that my health started to improve in more ways than I could have imagined. My skin began to clear up, I had more energy, I was sleeping better, and the best part was that my weight settled naturally where God intended it to be. After seeing all the positive physical changes, I became more mindful of how food affects my body and how good I feel when I eat nourishing foods.

In addition to feeling better physically, clean eating also allowed me to develop and maintain a healthy relationship with food and my body. Since adopting this lifestyle, I have been more in tune with my natural hunger signals, which allows me to feel physically satisfied throughout the day. I have now come to a place of balance in my life, and I am able to enjoy all things in moderation. This has freed me from counting calories and macronutrients—an unhealthy and obsessive act if taken to the extreme.

If this sounds like a far-off reality for you, I want to

encourage you. The reason I share my story in such detail is to let you know that there is hope! I remember being in such bondage to food that it caused me anxiety just to be around it...that is, until Jesus set me free. What I love about the Lord is that He is no respecter of persons (see Rom. 2:11). This means that what we see Him do for one person, He is willing to do for all. This means that He can and will bring you to a place of freedom as it relates to eating, just as he did for me.

For many of us, food has presented challenges that go far beyond making healthy choices. In this chapter we are going to dive into the different struggles that many of us have with food, and learn how to become satisfied in our body and soul.

I previously mentioned that I believe God intended food to be enjoyed. Not only did He take the time to make different types of foods, but He also gave us taste buds to enjoy them. Food is an essential part of our everyday lives, and it was created to nourish our physical bodies.

Unfortunately, many of us have lost the simple enjoyment of what God intended food to be, and have since developed a love/hate relationship with food. Just as with every good thing, Satan often twists God's very gift by preying upon our fleshly appetites. If we go all the way back to the Garden of Eden, where the first temptation took place, we can see how the enemy deceived Eve with the forbidden fruit. Many centuries later he tempted Jesus in the same way when he tried to entice Him to turn a stone into a loaf of bread.

After looking at the multiple accounts in Scripture where Satan targets the lust of the flesh, we would be wise to recognize that he isn't up to anything new, since he is still using the same method of temptation today. This is especially true for those who have struggled in the past in their relationship with their body or food.

Disordered Eating Versus Eating Disorders

Oftentimes when we think about bondage as it relates to food, we think of life-threatening eating disorders such as anorexia and bulimia. However, unhealthy eating behaviors manifest in many ways, and some are so common that we don't even see them as disorders. Although disordered eating may not be as severe as an eating disorder, I think it is incredibly important that we confront these unhealthy behaviors and bring them to light.

It is time that we call them out for what they are: bondage, the very thing Christ died to set us free from. Before we begin, I want to note that the list of disordered eating patterns in this book is certainly not comprehensive. In addition, the solutions I will be discussing are not to be used in place of a doctor's advice or care.

You may currently be struggling with an eating disorder. If this is the case, please seek the advice of a health professional as soon as possible. Don't try to use this book to break free from something that could be life threatening.

Also know that much of this chapter will focus on setting boundaries that relate to disordered eating, but that eating disorders are often addictions in which extremely unhealthy boundaries are already being used. Please do not use the advice listed here to validate boundaries that God never intended you to follow. We can fall into the trap of eating out of emotion or overeating, but it is just as dangerous (if not more so) to under-nourish your body.

God came to give you abundant life, but Satan comes to steal, kill, and destroy (see John 10:10). Recognize that starving your body just to maintain a false ideal is not healthy, and is caused by lies the enemy is feeding you to steal, kill, and destroy your life. If you are struggling in this area, tell someone you trust immediately, and be sure to seek the advice of a trained medical professional.

Emotional Eating

I want to begin by addressing some of the most common types of disordered eating among women I have worked with, as well as the disordered eating I have personally struggled with in the past. The first type of disordered eating is emotional eating. It is perhaps one of the most common, and it often stems from the need for comfort.

This type of eating can be brought on by myriad different emotions. Whether we are feeling tired, bored, stressed, sad, or lonely, oftentimes a bowl of chips or ice cream can seem like the perfect answer. The only problem is, shortly after the food is gone, we are often left with a sense of emptiness and guilt piled on top of the original emotion that we were trying to avoid.

A telltale sign that we are eating out of emotion is that we feel driven to food by something other than physical hunger. Specifically, emotional hunger makes us crave comfort foods such as cake, cookies, chips, or pizza. The urge to eat often comes on suddenly, and is a response to an emotional event or series of events.

When we eat emotionally, we don't just have a piece of

pizza because we are looking to fuel our bodies or because we are sitting down to truly enjoy it. Rather, that pizza represents a sense of control over our emotions, leading us to mindlessly indulge past the point of physical satiety while we're trying to stuff down our feelings with a temporary solution. The problem is, emotional hunger isn't satisfied when our stomachs are full. This type of eating often progresses into binge eating.

Binge Eating

Binge eating goes beyond overeating or having a second helping of food. It is the mindless consumption of large amounts of food to the point that one is uncomfortably full or even physically sick. Much like emotional eating, binge eating is often compulsive and is brought on by a void we are trying to fill.

The problem with both emotional and binge eating is that instead of freeing us from our emotions, they often pile on additional feelings of heaviness. After the food has been consumed and we come to our senses, we are still left with our original burdens, with the added bonus of a bloated belly and sinking feelings of shame and regret. To make matters worse, these feelings of guilt and condemnation often cause us to eat even more in what becomes a vicious circle.

Get Honest with Yourself

If you practice binge or emotional eating, one of the first things you can do to overcome is start asking yourself some honest questions. When you feel an emotional eating or binge eating session coming on, ask:

- What is going on in my life right now that is making me want to eat?
- What emotions am I experiencing?
- Will eating resolve my problem?
- How will I feel after I eat?
- And finally, how do I think God wants me to handle this situation?

Asking these questions will allow you to get honest with yourself and face your emotions head-on. It will also give you time to make a course correction and intentionally run to God instead of food.

I know this may be easier said than done in the midst of an emotional battle. This is because food provides instant satisfaction to our flesh, and it doesn't require anything from us in return. When we are feeling emotional, often the last thing we want to do is pour ourselves out in any way, so we turn to what feels good to our senses. At times it can even seem like a chore to run to God when all we want to do is tune out our feelings.

In moments like these, I have found that praise and worship are the best ways to soak up the presence of God and let His love wash away the emotions of the day. I like to go into a quiet room in my house, turn on some of my favorite worship music, and close my eyes while meditating on the lyrics. Sometimes I may just sit quietly, or I open my Bible and allow His Word to strengthen and encourage me (see Ps. 119:28). There are even moments when I start weeping as I feel the Lord strip away the burdens on my heart. It is in moments like these that running to God is not only the smarter choice, it is also one that leaves me feeling filled rather than drained even further, as emotional eating always makes me feel.

Jesus tells us, "To all who mourn in Israel, he will give a crown of beauty for ashes, a joyous blessing instead of mourning, festive praise instead of despair" (Isa. 61:3). I love this promise because it describes *praise* as a garment. When I turn on worship music or open my mouth and heart to praise the Lord, I picture the garment of praise being wrapped around me like a warm coat in a cold storm. Regardless of what is going on around me, I can put on the garment of praise, and it will repel the storm of a heavy spirit. When we are feeling heavy with distress, instead of running to food, or something that won't satisfy, let's turn to God and put on the garment of praise!

Setting Boundaries

Another way we can deal with disordered eating is by setting boundaries. This act can prevent emotional and binge-eating episodes before they even start! We can start by identifying triggers. A trigger is anything that causes us to go down a slippery slope with our eating patterns. These are different for everyone, so it is important to identify those specific to you. Some examples of a trigger point are a certain person or group of people, a specific environment, emotion, or situation, and even thinking about a certain type of food.

Once we have identified our triggers, we can set a boundary by staying away from those areas of weakness. For example, I personally didn't buy ice cream at the grocery store for a few years because I knew it would be a trigger for me. Instead, if I wanted ice cream, I enjoyed it with my husband while we were out on a date night. This allowed me to have a reasonable portion in a calm, relaxed, and safe environment.

Another way to stay away from triggers is by staying out of the kitchen altogether when you are feeling emotional. I learned to set boundaries in this way years ago, and it has helped me tremendously. If I am feeling overwhelmed or stressed (which has always been a trigger point for me), I pause for a moment and take inventory of my feelings. I don't allow myself to go near the kitchen in moments like these, knowing that things can quickly spiral out of control without warning. Instead I purposefully take time away with the Lord and allow Him to lift the burdens off my heart.

If you aren't able to stay away from a particular trigger for whatever reason, be sure to have boundaries in place to prevent unhealthy behaviors before they start. For example, let's say that your mom's house is a place where you find yourself looking for comfort food. Although you can't avoid going to your mom's just to escape an environmental trigger, you can have a plan in place to prevent emotional eating.

For example, you can decide ahead of time that you are going to enjoy a healthy snack before heading over. When you get there, you can sip on some decaf coffee or lemon water instead of snacking, which will keep you from the temptation to eat all the comfort foods your mom has prepared. If you are truly hungry, you can enjoy a small portion of food or a healthy snack rather than mindlessly eating just because food is available.

Making the choice to turn to God instead of food and

setting healthy boundaries are two powerful actions that we can take to walk out our freedom. It may seem difficult to make these changes at first, but we can trust that submission to the Holy Spirit, combined with action on our part, will always lead us into a place that is free from bondage and restrictions. It is for freedom that Christ has set us free, and by setting boundaries we are able to safeguard this freedom.

Dealing with Guilt and Shame

What happens, though, when despite setting healthy boundaries and turning to the Lord, we fall back into old sinful habits? When it comes to disordered eating, I have found that one of the worst parts of sin is the guilt that follows. Although it comes as a natural by-product of our actions, it tends to stick around for much longer than we expect.

The problem with guilt is that it often causes us to hide ourselves from God rather than turning to Him for help. For this reason, when we do feel that we have failed, we need to be quick to confess our sin to the Lord. The beauty of repentance is that it allows us to draw near to the Lord by faith rather than looking away in shame and regret (see Heb. 10:22). This results in a closeness where God is able to cleanse us from a guilty conscience, and we can come boldly to Him, asking for help in our time of need.

At times it can seem difficult to forgive ourselves, especially when we feel that we are frequently repeating the same offense. This is when we need to look at things from God's perspective rather than our own. One way we can do this is by looking up Scriptures on how Jesus set us free from condemnation, and asking God to help us see ourselves as He does. Although we may feel like a failure, God is a gracious and loving Father, and He promises to forgive us and cleanse us from all unrighteousness when we confess our sins to Him (see 1 John 1:9). We can receive the rich mercy of God as a gift with full assurance because of Jesus' blood that was shed for us on the cross.

Receiving God's forgiveness doesn't mean that we ignore our negative behavior or make excuses for why we sinned. Instead it means we take responsibility for our actions by turning to God, repenting, and receiving forgiveness for our sin. It can also be helpful to seek a spiritually mature friend whom you trust to hold you accountable and share your struggles. The Bible encourages us to "Confess your sins to each other and pray for each other so that you may be healed" (James 5:16). God never meant us to fight our battles alone, which is why it is so important to have someone to confide in and pray with.

God's Love Frees Us from Shame

I find it incredibly comforting that Jesus can relate to what we are going through when we are being tempted, although He Himself was perfect and without sin.

So then, since we have a great High Priest who has entered heaven, Jesus the Son of God, let us hold firmly to what we believe. This High Priest of ours understands our weaknesses, for he faced all of the same testings we do, yet he did not sin.

So let us come boldly to the throne of our gracious God. There we will receive his mercy, and we will find grace to help us when we need it most (see Hebrews 4:14).

When we go to Him with our sin, we can be confident that not only does He love us, but He understands what we are going through, and He has provided a way out.

We must remember that there is nothing we can do to earn His forgiveness. In fact, no amount of good works will ever make us good enough. It is by grace through faith in Jesus that we are forgiven. Renewing our minds with this truth reminds us to look to Jesus, Who paid a great price for our sins, rather than focusing on our weaknesses. When we see ourselves in Christ (forgiven and free), then our actions will follow. It is then that we are able to put off our old self and put on our new self, created in the likeness of God in true righteousness and holiness (see Eph. 4:20–24).

If after repenting and confiding in a friend you continue to struggle with shame frequently, I encourage you to seek a greater understanding of Jesus' love for you. His love for you is deeper than you could ever imagine. In Him you are adopted as a child of God, fully accepted and cleansed by His blood. As you seek out His love, I pray that you come to a place where you are able to shake off your shame and regret while embracing His promise to forgive, redeem, and renew your story!

Social Eating

Another area that disordered eating is commonly experienced is in social situations. Making healthy choices in a social setting can pose a challenge for many reasons. From holidays to social gatherings and celebrations, food is abundant when we gather together with others. To make matters worse, parties and get-togethers tend to have some of the worst nutritional choices available.

That being said, I don't believe that God is against us enjoying food as a way of celebrating or using it to bring ourselves together as a community. In fact, I think that the combination of food and fellowship was originally His idea! For example, we see stories in the New Testament where Jesus and His disciples broke bread together, often during their most intimate times of fellowship. Likewise, I am sure that we all have some amazing memories of being gathered around the table with family and friends.

In addition, many of us (including me) have a gift to serve others with food. (If you find that serving others food makes you incredibly happy, then you probably have this God-given gift.) Whether I am making a meal for someone who is in the hospital or preparing a meal for my husband or family, I love to minister to people's hearts while filling their stomachs. I also love to host people in my home as we share life and laughter and enjoy the gift of food together.

As you can see, it isn't a sin to enjoy food in a social setting or to give the gift of food to others. The problem arises when food, rather than fellowship with others, becomes the focus. While food is an element of a celebration, it should never be the defining factor or the most important thing.

Anytime we let food become an idol, it opens the door to temptation and sin. Some of the temptations that can come up in social settings are mindless eating, emotional eating, making unhealthy choices due to the fear of missing out, and succumbing to food-related pressure from others.

Overcoming the Setbacks of Social Eating

How, then, do we overcome the stumbling blocks that go along with social eating? I believe that the answer comes when we start to view food and fellowship according to God's original plan. I believe His plan always includes putting people and ministry first, making food nothing more than an enjoyable by-product of our gathering together. When our focus is on serving and loving others, our souls will be satisfied and food will take its proper place, which is simply to provide nourishment for our bodies.

Over the years I have learned various ways to combat some of the obstacles that come with social eating. Here are a few practical ways that you can enjoy food in a healthy way when gathering around the table with others:

Bring a healthy dish to pass. Eating healthy year-round (including holidays and special occasions) is possible. Oftentimes the hardest part is giving up the dishes you have had for years. Instead of giving up the foods you enjoy, I recommend making a healthier alternative and bringing it to the gathering instead. This also ensures there will be a healthy option for you to enjoy. Personally, I like to fill my plate with salad, vegetables, and healthier options (including the dish I bring), and leave the greasy and processed foods behind. For years I have been making healthier versions of holiday classics and bringing them to get-togethers. People enjoy them just as much, and oftentimes don't even know the food is healthy unless I tell them.

Learn that it is appropriate to say no. Social gatherings are often filled with a wide variety of foods that have been specially prepared for the occasion. This can lead to a false sense of guilt about turning down food. I have learned, however, that it is appropriate to be honest and say no when you've had enough to eat or a food doesn't appeal to you. It may seem difficult at first, but I have found that most people respect your decision when you politely say no. The great thing about this is that it allows you to say yes to the things you truly do enjoy. And you never know, you might actually inspire someone else to make healthier choices!

Plan ahead before gatherings. One way to prevent over-eating is by having a small protein-rich snack before attending a get-together or going out to eat. I find that this helps keep my hunger under control, which allows me to make wise decisions, such as passing on the bread basket and unhealthy appetizers. It also allows me to use proper portion control during my meal, as I am better able to listen to my body's natural hunger cues.

Plan for eating out. Before dining out at a restaurant I often go online to view the menu beforehand. This allows me to see what options are available and look for something that is reasonably healthy. Restaurants will often offer nutrition information, which makes it easier to choose your meal wisely. I try to look for a meal with around five hundred calories or fewer as a general rule of thumb, unless I plan to split an entree with a friend.

Learn to bounce back. If you do feel that you made a poor choice at a social gathering, it's important that you don't allow yourself to stay defeated. We must remember that it isn't one meal that will make us unhealthy; it is the sum total of our daily choices that makes a difference. When we get off track with our healthy lifestyle, we can make the simple choice to bounce back at the very next meal. I also like to start the next day by being active and making choices that fuel my body in a healthy way. *Making the choice to get back on track after a poor choice is what living a balanced life is all about.*

Change your focus. Although food is an element of a celebration, it should never be the main focus. I like to keep this in mind when I am on my way to a social gathering, reminding myself that time with family and friends is the highlight of the event. When we take our focus off the food, our attention will be brought back to the things that matter most.

Mindful Eating

In addition to helping me overcome some of the pitfalls of social eating, shifting my focus with food has been one of the most significant changes I have made in my overall relationship with my body. When I started to change how I thought about food, I began to look past my emotions and what my flesh wanted, and I started to think about the impact my choice would have on my body and soul. This allowed me to become more in tune with my hunger levels and shifted me into a state of mindful eating.

Mindful eating can mean something a little bit different for everyone. For me it simply means to be more aware of *what* and *why* I am eating. Instead of eating because of emotion, because of social pressure, or just to eat, I now make it my goal to enjoy food with the primary focus of nourishing my body.

One of the ways I have become more mindful in my eating has been by asking myself two important questions: "How will I feel as a result of eating this? Will it leave me feeling bloated and sleepy, or will it leave me feeling energized and fueled for my day?" I have learned that when I take a moment and think past my current situation, I am more likely to make a choice that leads to peace and prevents me from making choices I will later regret.

The second question I ask is, "Is this choice beneficial?" This allows me to properly distinguish if something is good for me or not. This is especially helpful in gray areas. For example, even though I know that some things are not necessarily bad in moderation, I have to ask myself if partaking of them will create an inroad for sin or bondage in my life, or take away from my health. Typically, if I am torn between two opinions, I decide if something is beneficial by asking myself, "Will this choice allow me to bring glory to God in my body and soul?"

For instance, I know that whenever I eat foods that are high in sugar, it creates a hypoglycemic response in my body. So because of my response to sugar, and for the sake of better health, I have found it best to abstain from sugar as much as possible. Because everyone's body is unique, we must ask ourselves how our choices are affecting our ability to do God's work.

These two questions have benefited my health in more

ways than one. They have allowed me to distinguish and overcome many unhealthy habits. For example, in the past I struggled with the temptation to eat late at night. I knew that I wasn't truly hungry because it was always after I had enjoyed a healthy and balanced dinner, and sometimes even dessert. Yet despite being physically full, I would find myself in the kitchen looking for a snack. Oftentimes it would be something like popcorn, chips, or another food I could eat mindlessly while relaxing for the night.

I was finally able to break this habit when I started to ask myself ahead of time how I would feel later on about my choice, as well as if it was beneficial. Asking these questions allowed me to be honest with myself and recognize that my choice to eat late at night always led to regret (in addition to a horrible stomachache in the morning).

After coming to this realization, I was able to set healthy boundaries for myself, and decided to set a "lights-off" policy for the kitchen after I had enjoyed my last meal of the day. After a few weeks of asking myself the questions, "How will I feel about this choice later on?" and "Is this beneficial?" I was able to break free of this habit once and for all.

That being said, as helpful as mindful eating has been in my life, I also want to be sure to set a proper balance. While it is important to be mindful, it is also critical that our thoughts don't become consumed with food, whether we're overcoming a disordered pattern of eating or simply learning to pay attention to our food choices. When most of our thoughts are about food (even if it is related to eating healthy), it can do more harm than good.

This is why it is so important that we keep our lives centered around Jesus, and ask Him to help us care for our body. This is best described in Matthew 6:25–27, where Jesus tells us, "'That is why I tell you not to worry about everyday life—whether you have enough food and drink, or enough clothes to wear. Isn't life more than food, and your body more than clothing? Look at the birds. They don't plant or harvest or store food in barns, for your heavenly Father feeds them. And aren't you far more valuable to him than they are? Can all your worries add a single moment to your life?'"

Eating as an Act of Worship

How, then, do we shift our focus off food while still thinking ahead and being mindful of our eating? We can do this by viewing food and eating as an act of worship! Jesus lived a life of worship because He walked with His Father daily, bringing Him glory with everything He thought, did, and said. I believe the first step to becoming more like Jesus is to pursue worship in every area of our lives, no matter how big or small.

When we have a heart of worship, we are continuously bringing all before Him, holding nothing back. It is in this place of surrender that He is able to free and deliver us from our weakness and temptations. For this reason I believe that worship is the ultimate path to purity in every area of our lives.

The Word of God confirms that this is true, even as it relates to our eating. 1 Corinthians 10:31 tells us, "So whether you eat or drink, or whatever you do, do it all for the glory of God." Whenever we focus on anything more than God, that very thing distracts us from our worship of Him, and it quickly becomes an idol. However, when we start to view eating and drinking as an act of worship, we shift our focus off food and onto the one true God. Suddenly something that was once selfish in nature becomes transparent and open to the light of His truth. It is then that we find true satisfaction, and the things we looked to for comfort (such as food) suddenly become worthless in comparison.

One of the ways that we can worship God with our eating is by asking for His wisdom every day. As we seek His will and treat our bodies as instruments with which to serve Him, we start to die to our sinful desires. Practically speaking, we can do this by taking a moment to pause and pray before we eat. By thanking Him for the gift of food, we are inviting Him to the table with us, and we are able to focus our attention on His guidance and leading.

We can also pray and ask the Holy Spirit to give us wisdom to know when we have had enough and when our bodies are properly nourished. Through this simple act, we are putting food in its proper place and viewing our mealtime as an expression of worship. Presenting our bodies as a sacrifice of worship unto the Lord brings a sense of thankfulness to our hearts. It is in this place of worship that He is able to satisfy the deepest longings of our hearts and lift any of the emotional burdens we may be carrying.

Another way we can worship the Lord with our bodies is by fasting. Fasting is repeatedly referred to throughout Scripture as a sacrificial form of worship and prayer. When we deny ourselves physical nourishment for a short period and turn our attention to seeking God, we are reminded that He is our true source of satisfaction. Jesus Himself invites us to find nourishment in Him:

> "Is anyone thirsty?
> Come and drink—
> even if you have no money!
> Come, take your choice of wine or milk—
> it's all free!
> Why spend your money on food that does not give you strength?
> Why pay for food that does you no good?
> Listen to me, and you will eat what is good.
> You will enjoy the finest food." (Isaiah 55:1–2)

In my own life, I have found that fasting causes me to die to my flesh and its sinful desires, and it also allows me to rest in God's nurturing care in an entirely new way as I reset my focus back on Him. (Please take note that wisdom must be used when fasting. For this reason I recommend seeking counsel from a Godly mentor before beginning a fast.)

If you desire to come to a place of balance and freedom as it relates to eating, take the first step by changing your focus with food. Instead of looking to food to bring a temporary sense of satisfaction, turn your eyes upon Jesus, who is able to fulfill the deepest longings of your soul. God's Word tells us that Jesus came to set the captives free (see Luke 4:18). If you believe this promise, you can believe that He will set you free from any kind of disordered eating or unhealthy habits.

Seek Him for wisdom on how to care for your body, and set healthy boundaries that will help you safeguard your freedom. As you worship the Lord and make Him your refuge, you will find that His presence fills you in a way that food never could. He loves you right where you are, right this very moment, and He is inviting you to taste and see that He is good!

FOOD FOR THOUGHT

Nourishment for the Soul

Scripture

For he satisfies the thirsty and fills the hungry with good things (Ps. 107:9).

Reflection Questions

- Can you identify with any of the disordered eating patterns that we have discussed in this chapter? If so, what are they?
- Have you learned any strategies for dealing with guilt as it relates to food?
- Do you find that social eating brings on anxiety about food? What are some ways that you can redefine social eating in a healthy way?
- How does changing your focus with food relate to worship?

Prayer

Dear Lord, I desire to come to a place of balance and freedom as it relates to eating. Help me to take the first step by changing my focus from food. Instead of looking to food to bring a temporary sense of satisfaction, help me to turn my eyes upon You, Jesus. Thank You for Your great love and forgiveness and for Your power that has the ability to set me free. Please give me wisdom on how to care for my body and set healthy boundaries that will help me safeguard that freedom. Father, help me to make You my refuge, knowing that as I worship You, Your presence will fill me in a way that food never could. In Jesus' Name, amen.

Nourishment for the Body
Taco Chicken Quinoa Bowls

These taco chicken quinoa bowls combine the best Mexican flavors and require only a few ingredients to make! Put a clean-eating twist on your tacos with this simple and delicious recipe!

Ingredients

Nonstick cooking spray
1 cup uncooked quinoa, rinsed (or uncooked whole grain rice)
1 (16-ounce) jar salsa (any kind)
1½ cups chicken broth (or 1½ cups water and ½ teaspoon salt)
1 cup corn

1 (15-ounce) can black beans, rinsed and drained
1 teaspoon garlic powder
2 teaspoons chili powder
1 teaspoon ground cumin
1¼ pounds boneless and skinless chicken breasts
1 cup shredded cheddar cheese (for topping)

Method

Preheat oven to 400°F. Spray a 9-by-13-inch baking dish with cooking spray. In a medium bowl, mix together quinoa, one-quarter of the jar of salsa, chicken broth, corn, beans, and seasoning. Pour into baking dish.

Top quinoa with chicken breasts and pour the rest of the salsa over the chicken. Cover baking dish with foil and bake for 30 minutes. Remove foil and sprinkle cheese over the top, then bake for an additional 15 minutes or until the cheese is melted.

Yields: 8 servings

10

STRENGTH TO RUN YOUR RACE

*N*ow that we have discussed caring for our bodies with nutrition, it is time to talk about everyone's favorite subject, exercise! I'm sure many people wish that I'd overlook this topic, or maybe forget about it altogether. If that sounds like you, I have good news! This is not going to be another lecture about how you need to work out six days a week or follow a plan in order to get fit. Instead, you may actually read this chapter and feel inspired to exercise. (Yes, that's right, I said *inspired*!) I can say this with confidence because I am approaching this topic from a personal standpoint, which means I completely understand what it means to dislike (or even despise) the thought of exercise.

My Personal Dispute with Exercise

Sure, I may enjoy exercise now, but when I was growing up, I disliked it with a passion. Growing up in a home with two sisters and a dad who wasn't into sports made it nearly impossible for me to be exposed to anything competitive or athletic in nature, which led me to be fairly underdeveloped in this area. This also led to a lack of confidence in my athletic ability, which caused me to dread anything sports related.

For example, I remember being terrified to play volleyball

in my fifth grade gym class. I was so insecure when it came to sports that instead of spiking the ball when it came my way, I ducked and dodged it like the plague! I still remember my gym teacher scolding me for allowing the ball to get away from me rather than playing the game competitively. My lack of confidence and ability caused me to hide in the back of the gym or sit on the sidelines the moment something became competitive.

Broadening My Horizons

Upon beginning my senior year of high school, I was informed by my guidance counselor that I must take at least one physical education course in order to graduate. My heart began to race and dread set in. As I began to panic, I pleaded with her to be an exception to the rule. The guidance counselor chuckled slightly at my dramatic response while assuring me that I did indeed need to complete one credit of PE. After hearing the reason for my dread, she suggested that I take an aerobics class the school offered. While I thought this sounded better than a gym class, I still cringed at the thought of anything that would make me sweat!

As it turns out, that aerobics class was one of the best things that could have happened to me, because it forced me to step out of my shell and get active! Through the class, I was able to try a wide variety of activities that improved my physical fitness (without the need for flying balls or crazy competition). That semester ended up being a time of growth as I broadened my horizons. I tried kickboxing, step aerobics, strength training, and even martial arts! Not only did that aerobics class allow me to try new things, it also helped build my confidence.

Out of the exercises that we participated in, I found that there were a few things I really enjoyed, such as kickboxing and strength training. I enjoyed kickboxing so much, in fact, that after I graduated I decided to look for classes in the area so I could continue pursuing it. That summer I found a class at a local gym, so I signed up for a drop-in class with my sister. The first class we attended was pretty nerve-racking, but we decided to stand in the back of the room and try our best. After a few weeks we started to feel more comfortable, so we moved into the middle of the room. Before we knew, it we were standing in the front of the class, beaming with excitement every class!

Looking back, I now see that the aerobics class was one of the best things that ever happened to me. It forced me outside my box to try something new. Exploring different avenues of fitness opened a whole new world for me and I found that exercise can be fun (yes, I actually mean *fun*) if you find something you enjoy doing.

Many different forms of exercise go beyond sports or the need for a gym. As I already mentioned, I enjoyed kickboxing because it was more like dancing than working out. Oftentimes the class would fly by and I wouldn't even realize that an hour had passed (or that I was sweating) because I was having so much fun learning the routine.

Over time, I started to branch out and explore different types of group fitness classes. I quickly found that these were a great option for me because they didn't require me to compete against anyone, and I could blend into the background until

I felt more comfortable. I also liked attending classes because the group atmosphere was motivating, and the teacher was able to encourage and guide me if I had any questions.

I tried a variety of boot camp and strength-training classes. These allowed me to work my body in different ways and learn the proper forms and techniques for lifting weights. Eventually these classes even gave me the confidence I needed to start lifting weights on my own, which helped build my strength and repair my metabolism after years of disordered eating.

Try Something New

If you are an exercise hater as I was, or you are currently doing something you dread, I encourage you to try something new. This may seem like one of the worst suggestions someone could make to you (remember, I've been there, so I get it), but it may end up being one of the best decisions you've ever made. (Please note, if you are new to fitness, be sure to check with your doctor before starting an exercise routine. From there, start slowly and build up. This ensures that you don't overtrain or strain your muscles, as it gives your body time to adapt and recover properly in between workouts.)

The great thing is, there are so many options when it comes to fitness. Many of the options don't even require you to leave your home, which takes all the excuses (such as a lack of time and resources) out of the equation! I recommend being bold and trying as many new things as possible until you find something that is enjoyable for you. That being said, it may not be enjoyable the first time, so be sure to give it a few tries before you move on to something else or give up.

Change Things Up and Find a Buddy

In addition to trying something new, I would advise switching things up as often as possible. Personally, I like to do a variety of classes at my local gym a few times a week, including a boot camp or a strength and toning class. I may even lift weights on my own or take an hour-long walk with my sister. I have found that changing things up helps prevent boredom and can help bust through a fitness or weight loss plateau.

Another recommendation is to find a workout buddy. I mentioned that my sister came with me to my very first kickboxing class, which gave me the confidence I needed to try something new. It was also nice to have someone there to keep me accountable on the days I didn't feel like going. Knowing that someone was counting on me gave me the motivation I needed when I felt like staying under my nice warm blankets at home. My sister and I still work out together, and we look forward to spending the time with each other.

Workout Options

Working out can and should be enjoyable, but it all begins with finding something you look forward to. Here are some examples of workouts to try:

Home Workout Videos: If you are anything like me in the beginning, and you are mortified at the thought of doing anything fitness related in a public setting, workout videos are great because you can follow them in the comfort of your own home. They are also great when you are short on time or if you have a limited budget. I recommend renting videos from your local library, or purchasing a few online. Many cable packages include great television options.

Group Fitness Classes: If you do have time to make it to the gym, but are feeling a lack of motivation to work out on your own, workout classes are the perfect solution. The great thing about group fitness classes is that they are generally geared toward every fitness level, and most instructors are great at offering modifications. Many gyms even offer the first class for free. If a group setting seems intimidating to start, you could also consider working with a personal trainer for a few sessions, or sharing a package with a friend.

Gym Workouts: Working out in the gym has many perks, and for some it is actually the ideal place to work out. Personally, I like working out in the gym on my own (or with my sister) on the days when I strength train. Many gyms offer a wide variety of different machines and equipment, which makes changing up your routine fairly easy. This can be beneficial when you are looking to beat boredom or a fitness plateau. On the days that I go to the gym, I like to have a routine prepared in advance. I find this helps me stay focused and efficient while I'm there, and I leave feeling accomplished.

Fun and Active: There are times when a traditional workout just doesn't seem exciting. In that case there are plenty of ways to get active outside of the typical gym setting, and it doesn't have to feel like working out at all. Below are some ideas to get your body moving both indoors and outdoors, if the weather permits.

Indoors: Dance classes, dancing around the house, indoor sports, cleaning the house, walking the mall, and playing with kids.

Outdoors: Biking, taking a walk, hiking, roller skating, canoeing, kayaking, golf (preferably without a cart) and other outdoor sports, washing the car, gardening, skiing and snowboarding, waterskiing, tubing, jumping on a trampoline.

Creating a Balanced Workout Plan

As you can see, there are so many different styles of exercise that there really is something for everyone! Once you find something you enjoy and you have been practicing it for a while, I recommend trying other types of exercise in order to get a well-balanced routine. This is important because different types of exercise emphasize different elements of physical fitness. Ideally, a well-balanced workout regimen should include two types of exercise: aerobic and anaerobic.

Before I lose you, let me put these two words into terms you may better understand. Generally speaking, aerobic exercise is any form of exercise that involves endurance-based cardiovascular training. This includes things such as walking, running, using an elliptical machine, and swimming. Anaerobic training involves strength-based activities that generally focus on increasing strength such as weight training, interval training, and circuit training.

It is important that we get a combination of these two forms of exercise, if possible, because they improve our physical fitness in two entirely different ways. Aerobic exercise increases our endurance and cardiac health, while anaerobic exercises help us build lean muscle mass, which improves our overall strength.

For me, finding a balance between these two types of

workouts has not only improved my health, but it has also given me the strength and stamina to make it through a busy day. I also like combining the two types of workouts because it allows me to change things up depending on what I have time for. I like interval training for the days when I have less time to work out, because you can get an incredibly effective workout in less than thirty minutes. I keep my longer cardio sessions (such as long walks with my sister) for days when I want to get out and enjoy the fresh air.

As much as I enjoy moving my body in an aerobic way, strength training has helped tone my body in a way that healthy eating alone never could. While it is impossible to change the shape of our body entirely (thanks to genetics), I feel that exercise has improved the appearance of my body overall by building lean muscle. While improved appearance should never be our only motivation to get exercise, it certainly is an added benefit.

While it's important to create a balanced workout plan, it is equally important to incorporate time for rest. Unfortunately, I learned this the hard way after taking my workouts to an unhealthy extreme. At some point in my journey I thought to myself, *If exercise is so good for you, why not do it every day?* Before I knew it, my four or five workouts a week had increased to six or seven intense workouts. With little to no rest time in between, this put stress on my body as opposed to furthering my health.

Six to seven days of exercise per week proved to be too much for my body. The strenuous exercise regimen caused me to stop having a menstrual cycle for years. I learned that when you don't give your body enough rest, it often interprets intense exercise as a physical stressor, causing more harm than good. For that reason, I always recommend taking a minimum of one to two rest days per week, even if you're at an advanced fitness level.

Staying Strong to Run Our Race

Even good things can be taken to an unhealthy extreme. While we know it isn't healthy to focus too much of our attention on our bodies, we must recognize that it is equally unhealthy to neglect our bodies through a lack of exercise. 1 Timothy 4:8 tells us, "For physical training is of some value, but godliness has value for all things, holding promise for both the present life and the life to come" (NIV). Notice that this passage doesn't say that we don't need exercise. Rather, it confirms that although exercise is good, it should never take precedence over our spiritual growth.

As long as we keep a healthy balance with exercise and keep the focus on improving our health, exercise can benefit us both physically and spiritually. The apostle Paul paints a wonderful picture of this in 1 Corinthians 9:24–27, which says, "Don't you realize that in a race everyone runs, but only one person gets the prize? So run to win! All athletes are disciplined in their training. They do it to win a prize that will fade away, but we do it for an eternal prize. So I run with purpose in every step. I am not just shadowboxing. I discipline my body like an athlete, training it to do what it should. Otherwise, I fear that after preaching to others I myself might be disqualified." In this passage the Christian life is being compared to a race that we must run in order to attain our eternal prize. Because we are spiritual and physical beings, we must keep our bodies strong in order to run our spiritual race here on earth with endurance.

You can see in our daily activities how our physical fitness may affect our spiritual race. For example, a strong, healthy body is better equipped to let us do our professional work and care for our spouses, growing children, and homes, and still have energy left over to minister to others.

Staying Motivated

In order to keep up with our physical fitness, there is one important requirement to get started and keep going, which is motivation. So how do we get and stay motivated when it comes to moving our bodies? First, I want to clarify that we all have days when we don't feel like pushing forward toward our goals. I too have plenty of days when I feel discouraged, overwhelmed, or too tired to exercise.

So the question is, on days like these, how do we stay motivated? Well, to put it simply, there are days when we have to exercise, regardless of how we feel, just as there are days when we don't feel like going to work, but go anyway because we are committed to our job, regardless of our emotions.

Let me give you a real-life example of this. Regardless of what is going on in my life, one day I may wake up and feel on top of the world, and the very next day I may wake up and feel terrible. This is just one example that demonstrates how emotions can be unstable, and therefore cannot be the basis of our decisions.

If we ever want to stay committed to something over the long term, we must be able to separate emotion from motivation.

If we relied on motivation to finish everything we started, we would end up leaving most tasks unfinished. You see, when we begin something, we often have a great sense of determination backing our decision. We often have a goal in our mind, filling us with so much excitement that we can almost taste the victory! Fast-forward a couple of weeks and here comes the decreased motivation, which often leads people to quit just shy of their goals. This change in emotions can have many causes: a lack of results, increased stress, or a realization that the process is harder or longer than we originally expected.

Staying Committed

Which brings me to my point. Instead of finding ways to stay motivated, you must simply make a commitment to do something and align your actions with that decision regardless of how you feel. I have learned to do this in many areas of my life. After praying about a decision, I make a plan and commit it to the Lord. From there, I set realistic short-term and long-term goals and write them down to keep myself accountable.

When I feel discouraged in my journey, I run to the Lord and pick up the Word of God. I encourage myself with the promises He has given me of success, and remind myself that He has amazing plans for my future if I remain committed and stay in His will (see Jer. 29:11). I also go back and reread my goals and reflect on the commitments I have made, which can be very encouraging.

Once I remind myself of my why, I make the choice to rein in my emotions and keep pressing on toward my goal. Sometimes I have to do this more than once, but the point is, I don't let myself remain in an attitude of defeat. I remind myself that I can do all things through Him who gives me strength (see Phil. 4:13, NIV), and I start to see myself as an overcomer!

It's also important to realize that your lack of motivation can be a tactic of the enemy. Satan would to love nothing more than to discourage you from running your race and pressing on toward your goals. You have to be aware of this and choose not to fall into that temptation. Instead you should keep Galatians 6:9 in the forefront of your mind: "So let's not get tired of doing what is good. At just the right time we will reap a harvest of blessing if we don't give up." This promise tells you that if you make the decision to keep doing what you know to do, the results will come!

My Top Tips for Staying Committed

Just like everyone else, I have days when I don't feel like working out, eating healthy, or taking care of my body. Yet, despite how I feel, I have learned to stay consistent, which is the key to results. Over the years I have learned a few things that have made sticking to my commitments easier. Here are some of my top tips for staying committed.

1. **Have a plan.** Specifically, I like to schedule my workouts ahead of time. I generally do this every Sunday for the coming week, so I know exactly what I will be doing on each day. I treat every workout like an appointment that I can't reschedule. This keeps me committed, even on the days when I don't necessarily *feel* like working out.

2. **Get workouts done early in the morning.** There was a time when I would have cringed at the thought of rolling out of bed and working out. However, I have found that there are often more pros than cons to morning workouts. I also find that it leaves little to no room for excuses when you work out early in the day. If you feel that you aren't a morning person, I recommend going to bed earlier. After a while, you may notice that working out first thing gives you more energy during the rest of the day.

3. **Be prepared.** One thing that has kept me working out consistently is being prepared. I like to have my clothes laid out, my workout bottle filled and in the fridge, and my workout written down (if I am working out on my own). That way I can set my alarm clock with just enough time to wash my face, brush my teeth, and throw on my workout clothes. Being prepared ahead of time allows me to get up and go, leaving less room for excuses.

4. **Eat a preworkout snack.** I like to eat something light before heading out the door for my workout. I recommend something higher in carbohydrates and lower in protein and fat. Carbohydrates are often the easiest foods to digest, giving your body the fuel it needs for the workout. I suggest something such as overnight oatmeal, fruit, or yogurt. Again, this will vary from person to person, so I recommend experimenting with a few different options to see what works best for you. Also, be sure to always have a water bottle ready to go. Being hydrated is especially important before you work up a sweat.

5. **Work out at home.** One thing that may be preventing you from working out is that you simply don't have enough time. If that's the case, there is a solution! Working out at home is one of the best and easiest ways to get a quick and effective workout because it doesn't require the extra time to get to and from a gym. There are plenty of at-home workout options that require only a few simple pieces of equipment (such as dumbbells), as well as some that don't require anything except your own body weight.

6. **Have a workout playlist ready.** A good workout playlist is one of the key factors that get me motivated to work out. Personally, I like to listen to upbeat Christian music while working out, which allows me to combine my workout with worship. This helps me start my day off on the right track physically and spiritually!

7. **Refuel with a healthy postworkout meal or snack.** If you do take the time and effort to exercise, be sure to fuel your body properly throughout the rest of the day. As important as working out is to our health, nutrition really is the most important component when it comes to maintaining a healthy weight and lifestyle. Personally, I have found that my body responds best after a workout to foods that are higher in protein and complex carbohydrates.

Be Patient

Finally, I want to leave you with a piece of encouragement. Despite all the information you've read, the thing to keep in the forefront of your mind is to be patient with yourself. Yes, it is possible to enjoy exercise, but it may take some time before you are really looking forward to it, or before you notice a change. Until you reach that place, I would encourage you to stay consistent and celebrate the small victories!

As with most components of a healthy lifestyle, change begins almost immediately on the inside, but it often takes time for it to show on the outside. For that reason, I encourage you to stay focused on the countless benefits of exercise that go beyond what you can see. As you stay committed, regardless of your feelings, stay focused on the small improvements. It will only be a matter of time before the little changes add up and you are able to celebrate your strong and healthy body!

FOOD FOR THOUGHT

Nourishment for the Soul

Scripture

No discipline is enjoyable while it is happening—it's painful! But afterward there will be a peaceful harvest of right living for those who are trained in this way (Heb. 12:11).

Reflection Questions

- Is exercise something you avoid? If so, what are some of the excuses that keep you from working out consistently?
- Out of the exercise options listed in this chapter, what are some you would consider trying?

■ Do you feel that you struggle with motivation when it comes to fitness? If so, what are some ways you can encourage yourself to stay committed?

Prayer

> Lord, I thank You that with You I can do all things! Help me to be determined to keep running the race and pressing on toward the goals to which You have called me. Please give me boldness and courage to try new forms of exercise, and give me wisdom about what the best options are for moving my body. Help me not to fall into the trap of discouragement and a defeated mind-set. I thank You that no matter how many times I fall, You will always help me get back up. I am making the decision today to keep doing what I know to do and I know the results will come as I make this decision not to give up! In Jesus' Name, amen.

Nourishment for the Body
Cheesy Chicken and Green Chile Lasagna

This is a delicious Mexican-style spin on a traditional lasagna. The noodles are replaced with corn tortillas, making it gluten-free, and it is mild enough for kids, making it family friendly! The best part is, it requires only a few simple ingredients, so it's easy to assemble for a busy weeknight dinner. For added convenience, it also makes wonderful leftovers and freezes well.

Ingredients

1½ cups shredded cooked chicken

½ cup reduced-fat cottage cheese (or softened cream cheese)

½ cup plain low-fat Greek yogurt (or softened cream cheese)

1 (4-ounce) can green chiles

1 teaspoon cumin

1 teaspoon chili powder

¼ teaspoon salt

½ teaspoon garlic powder

6 corn tortillas

1 cup shredded mozzarella cheese, divided

Method

Preheat oven to 425°F. Spray a 9-by-9-inch baking dish with cooking spray. In a medium bowl, mix chicken, cottage cheese, yogurt, green chilies, and seasonings until everything is just combined.

Layer 3 corn tortillas on the bottom of the baking dish. (I cut two of them in half so they layer more evenly, filling up any gaps.)

Follow the corn tortilla layer with half the chicken mixture, using a spoon or spatula to spread it evenly. Follow the chicken mixture with half the shredded cheese.

Repeat each layer, starting with the corn tortillas and ending with the rest of the cheese.

Cover baking dish with foil and bake in preheated oven for 20 minutes. Remove the foil and bake an additional 15 to 20 minutes, or until cheese is bubbly and lightly golden brown on top. Let cool slightly before cutting. Cut into 6 equal pieces.

Yields: 6 servings

11

ENJOY THE JOURNEY

As I shared in my personal story, I had to let go of countless things on the journey to health. Years of hurt, unforgiveness, burdens, and bondages needed to be uprooted and surrendered to the Lord. As I opened my hands and heart to Him, His Word and Spirit filled the holes that had been left by the deep and destructive weeds that once had me bound.

Along the way I remember praying countless times, asking God to take the pain and hardship away and release me from the bondage of disordered eating. Looking back, I'm so grateful He didn't deliver me in an instant, but rather took me by the hand and had me walk out my healing. It was there, in the journey, that I learned just how good God is, and how strong He is in me.

For so much of my life I was scared of letting go; I wanted control. But I finally came to the place where I knew that God's plans for me were good, and I needed to trust Him. In the process of surrender, I learned so much about Jesus and His incredible love and grace. It was in that place that I experienced His ability to heal, restore, transform, and make something beautiful from my pile of ashes.

I am still walking out my journey to health day by day, and will be as long as I am on this earth. I have the daily decision, just like everyone, to either submit to the desires of my flesh, which produce death and destruction, or follow the leading of God's Spirit, which produces life and peace within me. Each day, as I make the choice to put God first, renew my mind, and guard my heart, I am choosing life, and am filled with a peace that passes all my understanding as I grow stronger in the Spirit.

From the moment I began depending on God, my focus changed. Instead of thinking about ways to give in to my sinful cravings and desires, I now long to honor God with my body and worship Him with everything I do, think, and say. By no means does this mean that I am perfect or have everything together; in fact, the very reason I am writing this book is that I understand the struggle! I can now face areas of weakness without guilt or shame because I know that I am committed to His refining work within me, and that my imperfections ultimately reveal my need for Him.

Of course, I still have moments when I am tempted to give in to my flesh, just like everyone else, and I will be the first to admit that sometimes I do! In moments of temptation, I have learned that it is best to take action immediately and follow Jesus' example. So I open my mouth and begin to declare the Word of God boldly. Not only does this disarm the enemy, it also aligns my thoughts with the truth, which is half the battle. I also remind myself of my why, and think about the aftermath of the choice that I am about to make. Finally, above all else, I lean on the strength of God to pull me through, remembering that Jesus' resurrection power is inside me.

It is important to point out that I don't wait for temptations or problems to arise before I take action. Instead I do my best to build myself up spiritually every day, so when temptation does come, I am already armed with strength for the battle. I do my best to stay connected to the Vine and put on my spiritual armor, which includes reading the Word and praying Scripture every day.

I have been praying some of the same Scripture-based prayers for years now, while others I change up according to the season of life I am in. One of the prayers I wrote years ago is based on Ephesians 4:22–24, and I still pray it to this day: "Today I choose to put off behaviors and mind-sets that are according to my flesh. I put on my new self, created after the likeness of God in true righteousness and holiness. I choose to walk by the Spirit today and not after the flesh. I cast off the works of darkness and put on the armor of light. I put on the Lord, Jesus Christ, and make no provision for the flesh, to gratify its desires." I like to think of this prayer as a way to get dressed spiritually at the start of each day. It also reminds me that I have the ability to take off my old man (the flesh) and put on my new self, which was created in the image of God.

That being said, I want to clarify that my daily time with the Lord is not all about fighting spiritual battles. Rather, my primary focus from day to day is simply to spend quality time with my Heavenly Father, pursuing an intimate relationship with Him. When I sit down to spend time with God, I often spend a good majority of the time visiting with Him, thanking Him, asking Him questions, and soaking in His love. These times of fellowship are key to my continual transformation, because it is then that I can see my true reflection.

As far as caring for my body, I can honestly say that I have come to a place where I have learned to enjoy the journey! I focus on living a life of balance, which allows me to nourish my body and enjoy everything in moderation. For the most part, this means swapping out some of my favorite foods (that aren't healthy) with healthier alternatives, and limiting the amount of processed foods I consume, especially white flour and sugar.

I try to limit eating out to once a week, as I have found that it can be challenging to get a healthy and delicious meal at a restaurant. Plus, I honestly enjoy the food I prepare at home! When I do eat out, I choose a healthier option, such as a salad (with dressing on the side) or a source of lean grilled protein and steamed vegetables. When I indulge in something that isn't healthy, I choose carefully, picking something that I know I will really enjoy, like peanut butter ice cream. Then I make a point of sitting down and really taking my time enjoying it, without guilt, knowing that it is an occasional treat.

As far as planning, I plan my workouts and meals one week in advance, so I can be prepared for busy days and special occasions that may alter my routine. I start my weekly plan by choosing what meals I will make for the week and make my grocery list accordingly. Not only does planning keep my grocery bills down, but it also prevents waste. When I get home, I wash my produce, cook my protein, and prepare any pasta or quinoa I might be using in recipes. This way I have half the work done when I make a recipe or salad during a busy weekday. I also prepare something for a snack every other week (such as homemade protein bars or muffins). I store these snacks in the freezer and pull it out when I need a healthy snack.

I find that having a plan and being prepared is key to maintaining a healthy lifestyle in the long term, and the best part is, it gets easier with time! I also know from personal experience that in order to properly care for my body, I have to depend on God's strength, guidance, and wisdom every day. As I continue to care for my body and soul with spiritual and physical nourishment, I am able to walk in freedom and health, which keeps me fit for Kingdom use!

Seek First the Kingdom of God

As you can see, my journey to health had many twists and turns along the way, but my story always comes back to one thing, my unshakable faith in God. I have found that despite my circumstances or surroundings, my simple trust in a caring Father frees me from the nagging pressures and distractions of this life, allowing me to focus on what truly matters, which is the Kingdom of God.

Jesus reminds us of this truth when he says:

"That is why I tell you not to worry about everyday life—whether you have enough food and drink, or enough clothes to wear. Isn't life more than food, and your body more than clothing? Look at the birds. They don't plant or harvest or store food in barns, for your heavenly Father feeds them. And aren't you far more valuable to him than they are? Can all your worries add a single moment to your life? And why worry about your clothing? Look at the lilies of the field and how they grow. They don't work or make their clothing, yet Solomon in all his glory was not dressed as beautifully as they are. And if God cares so wonderfully for wildflowers that are here today and thrown into the fire tomorrow, he will certainly care for you. Why do you have so little faith? So don't worry about these things, saying, 'What will we eat? What will we drink? What will we wear?' These things dominate the thoughts of unbelievers, but your heavenly Father already knows all your needs. Seek the Kingdom of God above all else, and live righteously, and he will give you everything you need. So don't worry about tomorrow, for tomorrow will bring its own worries. Today's trouble is enough for today." (Matthew 6:25–34)

What exactly is Jesus telling us in this passage? I believe that He is saying we need to shift our focus off the things that this world holds valuable, and to seek those things that are on His heart. You see, despite all that we have covered in this book, everything comes back to this one thing: this life and everything in it are all about Him and the goal to further His kingdom here on earth!

Yes, it is very important to care for the health of our body and soul, and yes, it is important to fuel our body with life-giving nourishment, but at the end of the day, we have to trust that seeking after these things was never part of God's plan. In fact, I have found in my own life that when we seek anything more than God's Kingdom, it often becomes a distraction (or even an idol) as it draws our focus away from the things that truly matter. When it comes to our health, we must remember that the point of this journey is to experience the heart transformation that comes with seeking the Lord—which then works its way out into our physical bodies.

God created our spirit, soul, and body to be in accordance with each other, and when nurtured by Him, we will experience wholeness in each of these areas. This is why there is no need to be preoccupied with the worries, cares, and distractions of this life. We have a promise that if we seek His kingdom first, these things will be provided for naturally.

When we do our part to care for our health, He will give us the strength, guidance, and wisdom to do so. In turn, we will be able to effectively live out the purpose that He has called us to. The ultimate goal is to worship Him with our lives, which not only pleases Him, but also brings Him glory!

Have a Plan

So often in our journey to health, between our ever-changing schedules and life's circumstances, it can be difficult to stick to a routine over the long term. Combine that with the changes of seasons we all go through in life and it's no wonder many of us haven't seen consistent progress when we attempt change.

If this sounds familiar, I want to start by assuring you that it's never too late to begin again! No matter how many times you may have tried before and failed, you can be confident in the fact that there isn't anyone beyond God's reach or ability to change. Start by believing that He is able to deliver you, heal you, and set you free from anything that once had you bound. It doesn't necessarily happen overnight, but He promises to change us from glory to glory. If you do what you can do, God will do what you cannot do.

Despite how many times you have tried before and failed, know that there is a path that leads to victory, and it starts with having a plan! To make a plan that will last, I recommend using these five easy steps.

Write Out Your Plan

When it comes to writing a plan, the first thing I recommend is to set aside some time. Spend that time thinking through realistic goals, along with practical ways you can achieve them. (I suggest reviewing chapters 6–9 for practical ideas for nourishing your body and establishing your goals.) These goals may include things like developing a realistic workout schedule, clearing out your pantry, and establishing a plan to overcome mindless eating. From there, write out a routine that includes a daily, weekly, and monthly plan to help you get on track and carry out these changes.

Plan for Changing Life Seasons

Having a plan also keeps you from being derailed in your journey every time life turns in a different direction. Maybe you need to prepare in advance for something that could alter your daily routine, such as an upcoming project at work. Maybe you need to plan for something life changing, such as having a baby or sending your kids to school. By anticipating the different seasons in your life before they come, you can be prepared in advance for any pitfalls along the way.

Of course, there will always be things that you cannot plan for in life, which is why it is vital that you stay connected to the Lord. Keeping Him as the captain of your ship ensures that it will be safely navigated through the storms in life. That being said, if you are currently going through a difficult season and you haven't been connected to Jesus, all you need to do is call out to Him, and He will be right there to help you (see Ps. 107:28–31)! When the storms of life come my way, I like to remind myself of the things that God has brought me through in the past, knowing that He will be faithful to do so again. With Jesus in your boat, you can have peace and rest knowing that He will guide you through the roughest of seas.

Plan for Temptation

As you make a plan to overcome the obstacles you are likely to face, I suggest you also be proactive by choosing how you will respond when temptation comes. I recommend prayerfully considering areas that are weaknesses for you and writing out a plan to navigate them. (Consider reviewing chapter 6 and journaling about the areas of your life where you need to build your spiritual muscles.) When you are prepared in advance for how you will respond to sin and temptation, it has less of an opportunity to trip you up or make you fall. Also, you can be confident knowing that God has already provided an escape route for you.

Evaluate Your Plan

After starting a plan, you should take time regularly to evaluate if things are progressing in the right direction. If they aren't, it may be because you have set unrealistic goals that need to be modified. Most of the time, the only way to figure this out is through trial and error. In the meantime you can celebrate your efforts and redirect your course as needed.

Commit Your Plan to the Lord

All of that being said, a plan is useless if you don't commit it to the Lord. To ensure a successful follow-through, I suggest going to God in prayer before, during, and after you establish your plan. By committing your goals to the Lord, you are opening yourself up to His leading, guidance, and strength. If you get off course, He will gently nudge you in the right direction, and your plans will succeed (see Prov. 16:3).

Enjoy the Journey

As you walk along this journey to health, it is important to realize that your goal should be progress, not perfection. You can expect that your journey will be filled with highs and lows as you learn the arts of patience, commitment, and perseverance. It is also important to enjoy the journey!

One way of doing so is by finding foods that are both enjoyable to your taste buds and nourishing to your body. You don't have to eat kale and drink green smoothies in order to be healthy (unless of course that is enjoyable to you). If we are honest, most of us will stick to something in the long term only if we enjoy the journey, which is why I suggest finding healthier alternatives to your favorite foods. If pizza is one of your favorites, for example, find a recipe that is beneficial to your body and offers all of the flavor of pizza! (DashingDish .com is a great place for these kinds of recipes!)

I would also encourage you to change your focus with food. Start by thinking about how good your body feels when you are eating healthy, and let that be your driving force.

Instead of thinking about what you "can't" have, think about the ways you can improve your health and honor God with your body. By doing so, you are investing in your health and expanding your potential to affect His kingdom!

Second, find an exercise routine that you look forward to incorporating into your schedule. Try things that you never imagined you would, such as lifting weights, hiking a mountain, or running a race. It doesn't take long to notice the improvements in your health once you start exercising consistently, and eventually your energy levels, endurance, and confidence will grow in more ways than you could imagine!

Lastly, learn to enjoy the journey exactly where you are right now. One thing is for sure: when it comes to living a healthy lifestyle, we are all in different places on the journey. Some are just starting out and feel they have a mountain to climb, while others feel they have been going around the same mountain for years. Regardless of where you find yourself today, refrain from the temptation to look for the quickest route available, compare yourself to others, or strive for perfection. Instead, learn to celebrate the victories no matter how big or small. If you put on your tennis shoes and took a walk today, be proud of the fact that you have made one small step toward furthering your health!

Recognize that consistent daily choices that you make to improve your health count as progress in your journey and should be celebrated. In addition, keep in mind that while we will make progress, none of us will ever reach a place of total perfection in this life. In our journey to health, let us focus on one thing: forgetting the past and looking forward to what lies ahead. Let us press on to reach the end of the race and receive the heavenly prize for which God, through Christ Jesus, is calling us (see Phil. 3:13–14). As we do, we can be sure that God will enable each one of us to complete the good work He has called us to as we keep our hearts surrendered in childlike trust to Him.

We all get one life, one soul, and one body, each being a gift from our Heavenly Father, and He has given us the choice of how we will care for them. The good news is, He loves you, He is for you, and He has already prepared a way for you! God is asking you to take the next step with Him. Are you ready to embark on the journey? If so, let's pray this prayer together!

Dear Heavenly Father, today is the day that I begin my journey to health with You. I pray that You would take me by the hand and guide me, and that You would give me the courage, faith, and patience I need in order to stay the course. Regardless of my past, please help me to see myself as a new creation and have a heart revelation of just how loved I am by You.

Help me to divide truth from a lie, and uproot anything that may have bound me in the past. As I spend time in Your Word, I pray that you would cultivate the soil of my heart and that I would be transformed by the renewal of my mind. As I abide in Your presence, I pray that I would begin to see fresh life spring up from my soul. Help me to guard my heart and mind with all diligence, and to put off behaviors and mind-sets of the flesh. Help me to become strong in the battle, taking up my shield and sword and refusing to give in to any of the tactics of the enemy.

I pray that I would be filled with knowledge of Your will in all wisdom and understanding. And that You would give me wisdom on how to best care for the body You gave me. Help me to establish a plan that makes living a healthy lifestyle enjoyable and sustainable. And above all, I pray that You help me to see myself as You see me, and that I find my comfort, strength, and nourishment in You alone. In Jesus' Name, amen!

APPENDIX 1

Lies Versus Truth Chart

Lies We Have Believed	Truth from God's Word
I've tried so many times before and failed . . . I shouldn't even try to live a healthy lifestyle.	I will forget what lies behind me and push forward to the victory that lies ahead in Jesus. I will not be discouraged, for I know that I will reap a reward if I don't give up (see Phil. 3:13–14, Gal. 6:9).
I have had a hard day . . . My favorite foods will make me feel better.	Food won't bring lasting satisfaction; only Jesus can truly satisfy the longing of my heart (see John 6:35).
I like food too much . . . I could never change my eating habits.	I will not let food or anything else in this world have control or dominion over me. Instead I present my body to God to be used as an instrument of His righteousness (see Rom. 6:12–13).

It's my body . . . I can do whatever I want with it.	My body is not my own. It was bought with a price, and it belongs to God. I will not be mastered by my selfish desires or the lust of the flesh. Instead I choose to glorify God with my body (see 1 Cor. 6:12,19–20, Col. 3:17).
I'm too far gone . . . It would take years to get into shape.	Despite how I feel, I choose to be disciplined in caring for my body because I know it will give me the strength and energy to fulfill God's call on my life (see Heb. 12:11–13).
My body's appearance is flawed . . . I will never feel beautiful in my own skin.	My body was designed by God, who is the ultimate creator. I am fearfully and wonderfully made, every detail of my body designed uniquely by His hand (see Ps. 139:13–16).

APPENDIX 2

Scripture-Based Prayers for Your Identity in Christ

You Are a Child of God

Father, Your Word says that when I asked Jesus to be my Savior, I became Your child. The very fact that I am called your child demonstrates how much You love me. I thank you for adopting me as your very own daughter, and for bringing me into your family (see John 1:12, Rom. 8:15). In Jesus' Name, amen.

God Knows You by Name

Father, Your Word says that You know everything about me. You know when I sit down and stand up. You created and know me down to the smallest detail, even how many hairs are on my head. I thank You that You care about everything that matters to me, and that You delight in my sharing my heart with You. Father, Your Word says that You are close to me, even if I feel far away from You. I thank You that every moment of every day, You see me and You know me, and I am valuable to You (see Ps. 139:1–3, Matt. 10:30–31). In Jesus' name, amen.

You Are a New Creation

Father, Your Word says that You are familiar with all my ways, and I thank You that You call me pure and blameless despite what I perceive as faults and failures, and that Your love for me never changes. Father, Your Word says that You are merciful and gracious, slow to anger and abounding in steadfast love and faithfulness. I thank You that You love me with an everlasting love, and that in You I am a new creation. Help me to forget what is behind, and perceive the new things that You are doing in my life today (see Ps. 139:3, 1 Cor. 1:8, Ps. 86:15, Jer. 31:3, 2 Cor. 5:17, Isa. 43:18–19). In Jesus' name, amen.

God Cares for You

Father, I thank You that Your Word says You are always with me and that You are always in my midst. I thank You that You are my Mighty Savior, and You rejoice over me with gladness. Father, when I am busy, anxious, or stressed, Your Word says that you quiet me with your love. I pray that You would help me to slow down every day, and to be aware of Your presence and Your love for me. I thank You that I can cast all my cares on You because You care for me (see Zeph. 3:17, 1 Pet. 5:7). In Jesus' name, amen.

You Are Beautiful

Father, even when I don't feel pretty, You say of me, "You are altogether beautiful, my darling. There is no flaw in you." Help this truth become more real to me than anything else that I see, hear, or feel. Your Word says that true beauty comes from within, and although man looks at the outer appearance, You look at the heart. When I am tempted to see flaws and doubt the beauty You have placed inside me, I thank You that You will help me to see myself as You see me, which is beautiful in every way (see Song of Sol. 4:7, 1 Sam. 16:7). In Jesus' name, amen.

God Has a Great Plan for You

Father, I thank You for the great plans that You have for my life. I pray that You would help me to develop the gifts and talents You have placed inside me, and to use them for Your glory. Father, help me to trust You and acknowledge You in all my ways, and lean not on my own understanding. Help me to follow Your guidance, because Your Word promises that you will lead me along the best path for my life and that You will advise and watch over me. I thank You, Father, for going before me to prepare the way and for making my paths straight (see Jer. 29:11, Ps. 32:8, Prov. 3:5, Deut. 31:8). In Jesus' name, amen.

You Are Wonderfully Made

Father, I thank You that You created me in Your image. You knit me together in my mother's womb, and I am wonderfully made by You. I thank You, Father, for the great thought and care that You put into creating me. Thank You for the gifts and talents that You have given me to fulfill the specific purpose that You have for me. Forgive me if I have ever compared myself to someone else, or doubted the unique beauty that You have placed inside me. Help me to see the wonderful works of Your hand in every detail that You have created (see Gen. 1:27, Ps. 139:14, 1 Pet. 4:10). In Jesus' name, amen.

You Are an Overcomer

Father, Your Word says that whom the Son sets free is free indeed. I pray that You would help me to see myself as the overcomer that You have called me to be. I thank You for your Word, which has life, truth, and power in it to set me free in every area of my life. I pray that as I spend time studying it You will give me revelation of the truths that will set me free in my body and soul. Help me to walk by the Spirit, and not the flesh, for I know that Your Spirit brings life. I trust that You can restore everything in my life that once looked hopeless. I thank You, Father, that because You live in me, I am an overcomer and I am not bound to anything (see John 8:36, 1 John 5:4–5, John 8:32, Gal. 5:16, 1 John 4:4). In Jesus' name, amen.

ACKNOWLEDGMENTS

I would like to express my gratitude to the many people at the FaithWords publishing house who gave me the opportunity to publish *Nourish*. It has been an honor and blessing to work with everyone at FaithWords on this book. Thank you for investing in me and providing the ability to share what God has placed on my heart!

I would like to thank my editor, Keren Baltzer, and her assistant, Grace Johnson, for helping me in the process of writing and editing *Nourish*. I enjoyed every moment of working with you, and appreciate all the hard work and dedication you put into the process of shaping this book!

Last but not least, I would like to thank Blythe Daniel for believing in me. You have been such an incredible source of encouragement and support to me from the very beginning. Thank you for paving the way for me to pursue my dreams of becoming a published author!

ABOUT THE AUTHOR

KATIE FARRELL is the founder of Dashing Dish, a healthy-recipe website and ministry where she teaches women about their value in Christ. Katie is a registered nurse from Michigan, where she lives with her high school sweetheart and husband of eight years and their daughter, Madeline.

Katie is the author of the cookbook *Dashing Dish: 100 Simple Recipes for Clean Eating*, as well as a devotional book, *Devotions for a Healthier You*. Katie's mission at Dashing Dish is to inspire women to get healthy body and soul all while enjoying the journey!